EXPLORING

SPANISH

Second Edition

Joan G. Sheeran
J. Patrick McCarthy

Consultants
James F. Funston
Alejandro Vargas Bonilla

EMC/Paradigm Publishing, Saint Paul, Minnesota

with special thanks to:

David and Leslie Neira—musical editing, general
    and photographic assistance
James Douglas Sheeran—editorial advice
Judy G. Myrth—reading, editing, suggestions and
    other assistance
Mary Jo Horan—artistic inspiration
Jackie Urbanovic—illustrations
The Nancekivell Group—cover design
*Paul Renslo, Eileen Slater and the students of Oak-
    Land Junior High School*—photographic
    assistance
Christine M. Gray—desktop production
Christine Gensmer—project management

photo credits:

Mike Woodside Photography—cover
NASA—Earth
Feprotur—p. vii (br)
Christine M. Gray—p. viii (t)
Kay Jarvis-Sladky—p. viii (b)
Wolfgang S. Kraft—p. iii (b), p. vi (all), p. ix (all),
    p. x (all), p. xi (all)
Peru Tourist Office—p. vii (bl)
Rodolfo Reyes Juárez—p. xii (tl, bl)
Ned Skubic—p. iii (t), p. vii (t)
Spanish Tourist Office—p. xii (r)

ISBN 0-8219-1189-9

© 1995 by EMC Corporation

Published by EMC/Paradigm Publishing
875 Montreal Way
St. Paul, MN 55102

Printed in the United States of America
    6 7 8 9 10 XXX 99

INTRODUCTION

¡Hola y bienvenidos!

Hello and welcome! You are about to explore a world where hundreds of millions of people communicate in Spanish every day. For example, did you know that over 20 million people in the United States speak Spanish on a daily basis? Did you also know that Spanish is an official language of the Commonwealth of Puerto Rico? In addition, Spanish is the official language of 18 Latin American countries, the African nation of

Equatorial Guinea, and, of course, Spain. Because you probably will find yourself having to speak Spanish at one point or another in your lifetime, you are going to learn some common words and expressions in *Exploring Spanish* that are used often by native Spanish speakers. Then you will be able to understand some of the things they say, and they will be able to understand you.

If you practice correct pronunciation with your teacher or with the audiocassettes, you will learn to speak Spanish even better. Besides being able to understand and speak basic Spanish, you will find out some information about countries where Spanish is spoken and get some insight into their rich traditions in art, music, and literature.

Hopefully, throughout your journey you will discover that learning Spanish is fun and not too difficult. Be sure to practice your Spanish at every opportunity both in and outside of class. As with any other skill, the more you practice, the better you will become.

As the world continues to shrink and as countries and people grow closer and closer together, it is important to be able to communicate with each other. So, let's get started! *¡Vamos!*

Table of Contents

1 GREETINGS AND EXPRESSIONS OF COURTESY
Saludos y expresiones de cortesía 1

2 CLASSROOM OBJECTS
Objetos de la clase 8

3 CLASSROOM COMMANDS
Los mandatos de la clase 16

4 NUMBERS
Los números 20

5 GEOGRAPHY
Geografía 28

6 HOUSE
La casa 39

7 FAMILY
La familia 46

8 OCCUPATIONS
Profesiones y empleos 52

9 FOOD
La comida 57

10 ART
El arte 64

11 PARTS OF THE BODY
Las partes del cuerpo 71

12 CLOTHING
La ropa 80

13 TIME AND COLORS
La hora y los colores 87

14 MUSIC
La música 93

15 WEATHER AND SEASONS
El tiempo y las estaciones 98

16 DAYS AND MONTHS
Los días y los meses 106

17 LITERATURE
La literatura 115

18 LEISURE AND RECREATION
El tiempo libre y las diversiones 123

19 SHOPPING
Las compras 132

20 TRAVEL AND TRANSPORTATION
Los viajes y los medios de transporte 140

Exploring

...countries and cities

Mazatlán, Mexico

Seville, Spain

Argentina

Ecuador

Peru

...language

Puerto Vallarta, Mexico

Guadalajara, Mexico

...daily life

Madrid, Spain

Barcelona, Spain

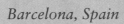

Lima, Peru

Barcelona, Spain

Santiago, Chile

Madrid, Spain

...and culture.

Guatemala

Spain

Guatemala

GREETINGS AND EXPRESSIONS OF COURTESY
Saludos y expresiones de cortesía

Buenos días.
Good morning.
Buenas tardes.
Good afternoon.
Buenas noches.
Good night.

Expresiones de cortesía

Por favor. —— Please.
Gracias. —— Thank you.
De nada. —— You're welcome.
Perdón. —— Excuse me.
Lo siento —— I'm sorry.

Hola. —— Hello. Hi.
Adiós. —— Good-bye.
Hasta luego. —See you later.
Hasta mañana. –See you tomorrow.

Sí.

¡No!

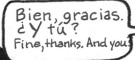

Buena suerte.

GOOD LUCK.

¿Cómo te llamas?
What's your name?

Me llamo Pedro.
My name is Pedro.

Hablas español, ¿no?
You speak Spanish, don't you?

Sí, hablo español.
Yes, I speak Spanish.

Encantado.
I'm delighted to meet you.

¿Cómo estás?
How are you?

Bien, gracias. ¿Y tú?
Fine, thanks. And you?

Así, así.
So-so.

¿Hablas español?
Do you speak Spanish?

No, no hablo español.
No, I don't speak Spanish.

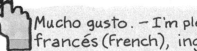

Mucho gusto. – I'm pleased to meet you.   alemán (German),
francés (French), inglés (English), italiano (Italian), ruso (Russian).

La cortesía mucho vale y poco cuesta.   Politeness is worth a lot and costs little.

Me llamo:

Amanda	Adán
Cándida	Alberto
Dolores	Andrés
Evita	Carlos
Francisca	Daniel
Guadalupe	David
Isabel	Felipe
Juanita	Francisco
Lucía	Guillermo
Luz	Jaime
Marisela	José
Mónica	Juan Carlos
Paloma	Lorenzo
Patricia	Luis
Pilar	Marcos
Raquel	Mateo
Rosario	Miguel
Sara	Patricio
Susana	Ramón
Yolanda	Tomás

Exercises

A Escoge la palabra que no pertenece. *Choose the word that doesn't fit.*

1. Hola.	Por favor.	De nada.	Gracias.
2. Adiós.	Buenas tardes.	Hasta luego.	Hasta mañana.
3. ¿Hablas alemán?	¿Cómo estás?	Así, así.	Bien, gracias.
4. Buenas tardes.	Encantado.	Buenos días.	Buenas noches.
5. inglés	francés	alemán	De nada.

B Escoge los nombres de las chicas. *Choose the girls' names.*

1. Cándida
2. Miguel
3. Adán
4. Luz
5. Carlos

6. Yolanda
7. José
8. Sara
9. Evita
10. Alberto

C Contesta en español. Escribe tus respuestas. *Answer the questions in Spanish. Write your answers.*

1. ¿Hablas español? _____

2. ¿Cómo te llamas? _____

3. ¿Cómo estás? _____

D Escribe al lado del dibujo la expresión española que pertenece. *Write next to each picture the Spanish expression that fits.*

1. _____

2. _____

3. _____

4. _____

5. _____

6. _____

7. _____

E Short answers. (En español, por favor.)

1. How do you greet someone in the morning?

   _____ .

2. How do you greet someone in the evening?

   _____ .

3. Two expressions at an introduction are:

   _____ .

4. How do you wish someone "good luck"?

   _____ .

5. Finish this sentence:

   Hablo _____ .

6. "¡Hola!" is used when addressing: (a) Paco   (b) el señor González

   _____ .

7. Spanish speakers sometimes shake hands to greet each other or to say good-bye. (a) Sí. (b) No.

   _____ .

8. Answer this question: "¿Cómo te llamas?"

   _____ .

9. "Good-bye" means

   _____ .

10. "Sí" is the opposite of

   _____ .

F Contesta en español. Escribe tus respuestas. *Answer in Spanish. Write your answers.*

1. Evita: Hola. Me llamo Evita. ¿Y tú?

   Adán: _____ .

2. Juan Carlos: Buenos días, Francisca. ¿Cómo estás?

   Francisca: _____ .

3. Juanita: ¿Hablas español?

   Patricio: Sí, _____ .

Crucigrama

G

Vertical

1. "...tardes."
2. I'm sorry.
4. Hi!
5. "Por favor."
9. "Good-bye."
10. "Me...Juanita."
12. "Mucho...."
14. "¿Y...?"
16. opposite of "no"

Horizontal

3. "...días."
6. "¿...estás?"
7. "Buenos...."
8. María says, "..."
   when she meets José.
11. "Hasta...."
13. "Buena...."
15. "¿Cómo...?"
17. courtesy

BUENAS NOCHES LE DESEA

hotel vista
aranzazu Guadalajara

Bienvenidos a este
paraiso llamado...

CARTAGENA

¡GRA
CIAS!

LARA CERVANTES PEDRO		
LERDO 236 SUR CP-63200		2-1193
LARA CONRADO FELIPA		
P MORENO NTE 68 CP-63200		2-1229
LARA RAMIREZ CARMEN PATRICIA		
FORTUNA 46 SUR		2-1648
LARES RAFAEL ARMANDO		
PROGRESO 207 CP-63200		2-0008
LARES RODRIGUEZ BONIFACIO		
MONTES DE OCA 409 OTE CP-60200		2-0334
LARES ULLOA SALVADOR		
PROGRESO 306 SUR CP-63200		2-0426
LARIOS FLORES SEBASTIAN		
MINA NTE 26 CP-63200		2-1235
LARIOS MONREAL FELIPE		
OBREGON 277 CP-63200		2-0560
LARIOS MONREAL RICARDO		
ALVARO OBREGON 504 CP-63200		2-2312
LARRERA ROMERO FERNANDO		
ZARAGOZA 109 SUR CP-63200		2-2095
LAU CAU MANUEL		
INDEPENDENCIA Y MORELOS		
CP-63200		2-0052
LEAL BUENO CONSUELO		
MADERO 119 SUR CP-63200		2-0248
LEAL BUENO JULIO		
VICTORIA SUR 6 CP-63200		2-0420
LEAL JIMENEZ MARIANO		
MAZATLAN OTE 605 CP-63200		2-0403
LEAL MAYORGA MA DEL ROSARIO		
J ESCUTIA 602 CP-63200		2-1304
LEDEZMA ARAMBURO MA VIANEY		
CORONA OTE 1399 CP-63200		2-1072
LEDON ALCARAZ ROBERTO		
CONSTITUCION 8 NTE CP-63200		2-0048
LEDON CRESPO FRANCO		
FORTUNA 26 NTE CP-63200		2-1018
LEDON GONZALEZ LUIS		
INDEPENDENCIA OTE 606 CP-63200		2-1106
LEMUS DELGADO FLORA		
CONSTITUCION SUR 131 CP-63200		2-0393
LEMUS SANDOVAL BASILIO		
CORONA 795 OTE CP-63200		2-1683
LEMUS SANDOVAL JOSE LUIS		
PROLG CORONA 781 CP-63200		2-1374
LEMUS VILLAGRANA DIONISIA		
J ESCUTIA 1301 CP-63200		2-0728
LEON LLAMAS ESTEBAN		
REFORMA 86 CP-63200		2-0464
LERMA JIMENEZ SANTIAGO		
CONSTITUCION NTE 33 CP-63200		2-1177
LEYVA DE LA CRUZ MA GUADALUPE		
HIDALGO 403 OTE CP-63200		2-2112
LEYVA RIVERA MARIA		
MINA 165 SUR CP-63200		2-2163
LICORERIA CENTRAL		
HIDALGO 55-A CP-63200		2-0122
LINARES RAMOS MA DEL ROSARIO		
ITURBIDE 410 SUR CP-63200		2-1655
LINEA BLANCA HUERTA		
MADERO 302 SUR CP-63200		2-0050
LIRA MARTINEZ SALVADOR DE		
CORONA 1106 CP-63200		2-0387
LIZARRAGA LARA FRANCISCO		
N MENDOZA 115 CP-63200		2-1355
LIZARRAGA MONTERO CONRADO		
PUEBLA E INDEPENDENCIA 910		
CP-63200		2-1473
LIZARRAGA MONTERO GUALBERTO		
S		
PUEBLA 104 SUR CP-63200		2-2158
LOMELI HERNANDEZ SOLEDAD		
LIBERTAD 1004 OTE CP-63200		2-1554
LOMELI SALAZAR FRANCISCA		
CORONA 412 PTE CP-63200		2-1495
LOMELI VERDIN ARCELIA		
PUEBLA SUR 219 CP-63200		2-1389
LONCHERIA CRESPO		
HIDALGO OTE 67 CP-63200		2-0675
LOPEZ ACOSTA JESUS		
CORONA 420 PTE CP-63200		2-1528
LOPEZ BETANCOURT TORIBIO		
MINA 49 SUR CP-63200		2-1949
LOPEZ BOJORQUEZ EFREN		
JUAREZ 15 OTE CP-63200		2-1558
LOPEZ CALVILLO PATRICIA		
INDEPENDENCIA OTE 1322 CP-63200		2-1125
LOPEZ CARDENAS RITO		
JUAN ESCUTIA 1504 OTE CP-63200		2-1844
LOPEZ CARDENAS ROSALVA		
LIBERTAD 1503 CP-63200		2-1479
LOPEZ CLARA		
HIDALGO 106 OTE CP-63200		2-0011
LOPEZ CORDERO ESTHER		
MEXICO SUR 709 CP-63200		2-1056
LOPEZ CUETO MERCEDES		
CORONA 505 PTE CP-63200		2-1486
LOPEZ CUEVA FELIPE		
BRAVO 18 NTE CP-63200		2-0601
LOPEZ DE DIOS ANDREA		
CORONA 204 PTE CP-63200		2-2216
LOPEZ FABRY JOSE LUIS		
REFORMA 400 SUR CP-63200		2-1408
LOPEZ FRANCO JOSE CARMEN		
INDEPENDENCIA 718 PTE CP-63200		2-0671
LOPEZ GARCIA JOSE		
FCO SARABIA 299 CP-63200		2-1830
LOPEZ GARCIA MA CARMEN		
CONSTITUCION 508-BIS SUR CP-63200		2-1181
LOPEZ GARCIA RICARDA PROFA		
P MORENO SUR 126 CP-63200		2-1118
LOPEZ GONZALEZ TRINIDAD		
JUAREZ 910 PTE CP-63200		2-2013
LOPEZ GUERRERO CELIA		
HIDALGO 519 PTE CP-63200		2-1720
LOPEZ GUZMAN APOLONIO		
MINA 28 NTE CP-63200		2-0314
LOPEZ IBARRA ESPERANZA		
HIDALGO OTE 6 CP-63200		2-0316
LOPEZ JAIME MARTINIANO		
QUERETARO 309 CP-63200		2-1491
LOPEZ JIMENEZ JUANA		
JUAREZ Y ZAPATA 1201 CP-63200		2-1734
LOPEZ JIMENEZ LUCRECIA		
S ROCHA 21 CP-63200		2-0563
LOPEZ LLANOS MA GUADALUPE		
LERDO 222 CP-63200		2-2258
LOPEZ MALDONADO SALVADOR		
MONTES DE OCA 804 OTE CP-63200		2-0131
LOPEZ MENDEZ FERNANDO		
INDEPENDENCIA 1118 OTE CP-63200		2-0734
LOPEZ MITRE BELEN		
CUAUHTEMOC 51 CP-63645		2-2335
LOPEZ MONTES CATALINA		
BERNARDO OROSCO 48 CP-63200		2-0755
LOPEZ OROZCO MARIA GLORIA		
J ESCUTIA OTE 1007 CP-63200		2-1127
LOPEZ PARTIDA RENE G PROF		
HIDALGO PTE 504 CP-63200		2-0361
LOPEZ PEÑA FRANCISCO		
MADERO 118 SUR CP-63200		2-0243
LOPEZ PRECIADO J JESUS		
MEXICO 125 SUR CP-63200		2-0331

LOPEZ RAMIREZ JESUS		
CARRANZA 305-A CP-63200		2-1065
LOPEZ RAYGOZA MIGUEL ANGEL		
JUAN ESCUTIA 402 PTE CP-63200		2-1582
LOPEZ RENTERIA FIDEL		
COLONIA E ZAPATA J 9 CP-63200		2-1702
LOPEZ RODRIGUEZ VALENTIN		
VALERIO TRUJANO 35 CP-63200		2-2277
LOPEZ SALAS AGUSTINA		
MINA Y CORONA 52 SUR CP-63200		2-1773
LOPEZ SANTOYO BERNARDINO		
INDEPENDENCIA Y FCO SARABIA		
CP-63000		2-1599
LOPEZ T CRESCENCIANO		
COL E ZAPATA MANZ P LTE 1		
CP-63200		2-0281
LOPEZ VEGA MA DEL REFUGIO		
JUAREZ 110 PTE CP-63200		2-0093
LOPEZ VERDE MA NATIVIDAD		
MANUEL URIBE 81 CP-63200		2-1710
LOPEZ VERDIN LUIS ANTONIO		
CONSTITUCION 216 SUR CP-63200		2-1780
LOPEZ VILLA MARINA		
MONTES DE OCA 400 CP-63200		2-0312
LOZANO DELGADO OCTAVIO		
CORONA 309 PTE CP-63200		2-1825
LUCIO CEJA GODOY		
HIDALGO 913 PTE CP-63200		2-1835
LUEVANO NAJAR PAULA		
FRANCISCO I MADERO 417 SUR		
CP-63200		2-1471
LUNA DE DIOS FELIPE		
JUAN ESCUTIA 111 OTE CP-63200		2-1485
LUNA ESCAMILLA A PATRICIA		
CENTENARIO 201-A CP-63200		2-1347
LUNA FIGUEROA JOSE ILDEFONSO		
HIDALGO 100 PTE CP-63200		2-1848
LUNA LOPEZ JORGE ALEJANDRO		
FORTUNA 119 SUR CP-63200		2-0825
LUNA ORNELAS ARMANDO		
CENTENARIO 203 SUR CP-63200		2-0076
EDUARDO AUDELO 6 CP-63200		2-2048
LUNA PARTIDA MISAEL		
MONTES DE OCA 404-BIS CP-63200		2-0304

LL

LLAMAS ESCOBEDO NATIVIDAD		
BRAVO SUR 241 CP-63200		2-1136
LLAMAS LOPEZ MA DE LA LUZ		
NARCIZO MENDOZA 68 CP-63200		2-2231
LLANTAS GOOD YEAR OXO DE		
TUXPAN		
HIDALGO Y FORTUNA CP-63200		2-0058

M

M GUZMAN MORA MANUEL		
EMILIO CARRANZA 84 SUR CP-63200		2-1715
MA DEL ROCIO GONZALEZ ULLOA		
COL E ZAPATA MANZANA P 6		
CP-63200		2-1598
MACHAIN DELGADO J CRUZ		
HIDALGO 408 PTE CP-63200		2-0218
MACIAS CARRILLO SOFIA		
COL E ZAPATA MANZ K No 2		
CP-63200		2-1274
MACIAS DELGADILLO MELECIO		
CORONA 725 CP-63200		2-1733
MACIAS ROBLES JOSE GUADALUPE		
F SARABIA SUR 292 CP-63200		2-1315
MACIAS SALMERON J TRINIDAD		
F SARABIA 283 CP-63200		2-0397
MACIAS VENEGAS JUANA		
CORONA 133 PTE CP-63200		2-0127
MACIAS ZEPEDA CANDELARIO		
MINA 83 NTE CP-63200		2-1999
MADERA RAMIREZ ALBA ELENA		
LIBERTAD 123 PTE CP-63200		2-1549
MADERAS DE CHIHUAHUA EN		
TUXPAN NAY		
CONSTITUCION 266 SUR CP-63200		2-0318
MADERERIA LIZARRAGA		
INDEPENDENCIA OTE 814 CP-63200		2-1079
MADRIGAL ARANGURE MA DEL		
REFUGIO		
JUAREZ 615 PTE CP-63200		2-2037
MAGANA VAZQUEZ MA GUADALUPE		
LIBERTAD OTE 1212 CP-63200		2-0692
MAGALLANES VALENCIA MA		
CONCEPCION		
PUEBLA SUR 104 CP-63200		2-1180
MAGDALENA CARRANZA RAMOS		
JUAN ESCUTIA 1204 OTE CP-63200		2-2315
MAISTERRA MAISTERRA PEDRO		
HIDALGO 119 ORIENTE CP-63200		2-0007
MAISTERRA MORONES ENRIQUE		
PUEBLA 218 SUR CP-63200		2-1684
MALDONADO EVANGELISTA MA		
JOSEFINA		
D CARMONA S-N CP-63200		2-1459
MALDONADO FELIX MARIA		
LIBERTAD 870 CP-63200		2-1896
MALDONADO FELIX RAMONA		
QUERETARO SUR 208 CP-63200		2-1398
MALDONADO JUAREZ ANTONIO		
MEXICO SUR 714 CP-63200		2-0700
MALDONADO SANCHEZ MA ISABEL		
QUERETARO SUR 122 CP-63200		2-0514
MAQUINARIA INTERCONTINENTAL DE		
OCCI		
HIDALGO Y MEXICO CP-63600		2-1399
MARENTES HERRERA OLGA ALICIA		
ANACLETO CORREA 405 OTE		2-2201
MARIACHI LOS CARDENALES		
MEXICO 300A CP-63200		2-1396
MARIN GONZALEZ JOSE		
LERDO DE TEJADA SUR 188 CP-63200		2-1352
MARIN MARTINEZ GONZALO		
LIBERTAD 77 PTE CP-63200		2-0702
MARISCAL CUEVAS FELIPE		
MORELOS 191 SUR CP-63200		2-0524
MARMOLEJO PARRA S TRINIDAD		
NARCIZO MENDOZA Y LERDO		
CP-63200		2-1790
MARQUEZ ALCARAZ ALEJANDRO		
LEON VICARIO 60 NTE CP-63200		2-1762
MARQUEZ SOLIS CONCEPCION		
LAURELES 600 CP-63200		2-0071
MARRUJO SEBASTIANA QUINTERO		
DE		
E CARRANZA SUR 303 CP-63200		2-0857
MARTHA ORNELAS CASTORENA		
MONTES DE OCA 709 CP-63200		2-1576

CLASSROOM OBJECTS
Objetos de la clase

2

¿Qué es esto?
Es un...
Es una...

What's this?
It's a....

una pared
a wall

un mapa   a map

una clase
a classroom, class

una ventana
a window

un cuadro

un reloj
a clock

una
punta
a point

un lápiz

una
goma
an eraser

un
sacapuntas
a pencil
sharpener

una bandera
a flag

una pizarra   a board

a pencil

a picture

una
silla
a chair

un borrador
an eraser

una tiza
a chalk

un
escritorio
a desk

un estante de libros
a bookcase

un libro
a book

un papel
a paper

un cuaderno
a notebook

una
papelera
a wastebasket

un bolígrafo
a ballpoint pen

una regla
a ruler

un pupitre
a desk

"Boli" is the short form of "bolígrafo."

Es mejor evitar que remediar.   An ounce of prevention is
worth a pound of cure.

8

Exercises

A Listening Comprehension

Your teacher will point out twenty-four classroom objects. As he or she pronounces the name of each in Spanish, find it on the list below and place the appropriate number after it.

una bandera __14__   un estante de libros __5__
un libro __7__   una clase __23__
una tiza __20__   un escritorio __8__
un cuaderno __22__   una papelera __15__
un bolígrafo __2__   una silla __18__
un lápiz __16__   una goma __24__
una pizarra __10__   una pared __1__
un borrador __13__   un papel __17__
un mapa __4__   una punta __9__
una regla __19__   una ventana __21__
un cuadro __6__   un sacapuntas __11__
un pupitre __12__   un reloj __3__

B Answer each question in English.

1. Where in the classroom is the "bandera"?

_____

2. What is indicated by the "reloj"?

_____

3. What is hung on a "pared" to decorate a room?

_____

C Escoge la respuesta correcta. *Choose the correct response.*

1. One writes on the "pizarra" with....
   a. chalk   b. a pencil
2. Light enters through the....
   a. silla   b. ventana
3. The (chalk)board is cleaned with a....
   a. goma   b. borrador
4. The "sacapuntas"....
   a. sharpens pencils   b. makes chalk
5. Waste materials are deposited in the....
   a. pupitre   b. papelera

D Escribe en español la palabra o frase que corresponde a cada dibujo. *Write the Spanish word or phrase that corresponds to each picture.*

1. _____

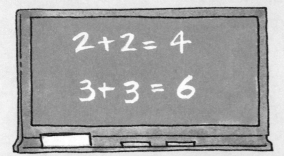

2. _____

3. _____

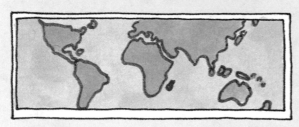

4. _____

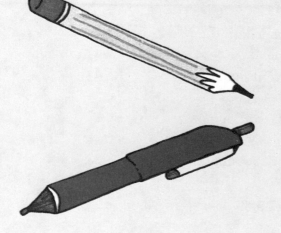

5. _____

6. _____

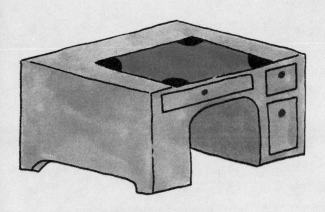

7.  _____

8. _____

9. _____

10. _____

11. _____

12. _____

13. _____

14. _____

15. _____

E Completa las frases. *Fill in the missing words.*

1. ¿_____ es esto?

2. _____ un bolígrafo.

3. Es _____ papelera.

4. Es _____ borrador.

F Escribe la letra que falta. *Write the missing letter.*

1. l__piz

2. cua__erno

3. __apel

4. sill__

5. es__ante de libros

6. bo__ígrafo

7. r__loj

8. __uadro

9. pape__era

10. p__pitre

11. __apa

12. v__ntana

13. pun__a

14. tiz__

15. clas__

16. borra__or

17. band__ra

18. g__ma

19. reg__a

20. __acapuntas

21. par__d

22. p__zarra

23. __scritorio

24. li__ro

Crucigrama

G

Vertical

1. written on with pen or pencil
2. makes a point
3. notebook
5. the teacher's desk
7. outline of a country
9. needs sharpening
10. garbage receptacle
11. where pupil works
12. group of students
14. cleans (chalk)boards
18. used to write on the board

Horizontal

4. window
6. male student's name: Michael
8. place to sit
10. writing instrument (*short form*)
13. measures things
15. used with chalk
16. read by student
17. holds books ("...de libros")
19. removes errors

Cuaderno Profesional P.S.G.
Rayado, Cuadros
Chico y Grande,
100 Hojas N$ 3.⁴⁰

Cinta Adhesiva
P.S.G. 12x10 80¢
Transparente

Cinta Adhesiva
P.S.G. 12x20 N$ 1.⁵⁰
Transparente

Masking Tape
P.S.G. 12x10 N$ 1.⁶⁰

Masking Tape
P.S.G. 12x25 N$ 2.⁵⁰

Lamparas
Para Escritorios
30%

Despertadores
y Relojes
30%

Disketts para
Computadora
30%

Escritorios 30%

Pritt Lápiz Adhesivo
con Sacapuntas
3.⁵⁰

Todos los
Bolígrafos 30%
Importados

Todos los
Sacapuntas 30%
Nacionales e Importados

CLASSROOM COMMANDS
Los mandatos de la clase

Repite.
Repeat.

Contesta la pregunta.
Answer the question.

Habla.
Speak.

Dilo en español.
Say it in Spanish.

Levanta la mano.
Raise your hand.

Saca papel.
Take out paper.

Abre el libro.
Open the book.

Cierra el libro.
Close the book.

Escribe.
Write.

Escucha.
Listen.

Lee.
Read.

Siéntate.
Sit down.
Be seated.

Completa las frases.
Complete the sentences.

Pasa a la pizarra.
Go to the board.

 A palabras necias, oídos sordos.

To foolish words lend a deaf ear.

Exercises

A Do what your teacher commands.

B Escribe en español, por favor. *Write in Spanish, please.*

1. (Speak.) _____

2. (Say.) _____

3. (Answer.) _____

C Do as the following command says.

Escribe <u>tu nombre completo</u>. _____
          (your complete name)

D Asocia la frase en inglés con la palabra en español. *Match the English with the Spanish.*

A		B
1. abrir _____		a. to write
2. contestar _____		b. to open
3. escribir _____		c. to speak
4. cerrar _____		d. to answer
5. hablar _____		e. to close

E Escribe un mandato en español para cada dibujo. *Write a Spanish command for each picture.*

1. _____

2. _____

3. _____

4. _____

5. _____

F Completa cada frase en español. *Complete each sentence in Spanish.*

1. _____ papel.

2. Levanta la _____.

3. _____ la pregunta.

4. Dilo en _____.

5. _____ a la pizarra.

6. Completa las _____.

7. _____ el libro.

G En cada grupo escoge el mandato correcto. *Choose the correct command in each group.*

1. Speak. (Lee.   Repite.   Habla.)
2. Answer. (Completa. Contesta. Abre.)
3. Listen. (Dilo.   Escribe.   Escucha.)
4. Write. (Escribe.   Lee.   Escucha.)
5. Read. (Lee   Pasa.   Saca.)

EXPOSOCIAL

Transformará su comunidad
Vivienda Social, Desarrollo Comunitario
y Economía Solidaria.

Venga!
Es por un Bien Común.

Di NO

a las
drogas

Quien llama primero gana

LLAMA O GANA!

CON SÚPER 6 SEIS

a partir del 2 de agosto

El deporte
es básico
PARA
la salud.
Practícalo!.

EN EL PARTIDO DE HOY

ESCUCHE A LOS QUE SABEN

ESCUCHE A LOS QUE SIENTEN

ESCUCHE CARACOL

dibújeme
Y GANE
UNA BECA

para
estudiar
seriamente

DIBUJO
(TODAS LAS
ESPECIALIDADES)

Si no desea desprender la
hoja puede remitir el dibujo
y los datos que se solicitan
en el cupón en hoja
aparte mencionando
esta revista.

Efectúe este dibujo sin demora
(puede usar lápiz, bolígrafo o tinta).
Recorte el anuncio y remítalo sin
tardanza. SU DIBUJO será juzgado
y si Ud. realmente tiene posibilida-
des en este fabuloso campo le otor-
garemos...

REMITA
EL CUPÓN Y EL
DIBUJO HOY MISMO
OFERTA
POR TIEMPO
LIMITADO

UNA BECA PARA ESTUDIAR EL MEJOR
CURSO DE DIBUJO DEL MUNDO!...

Llame
Consulte
Compre

4 NUMBERS
Los números

¿Cuánto es...? How much is...?
¿Cuántos son...? How many are...?

1 uno
2 dos
3 tres
4 cuatro
5 cinco

6 seis
7 siete
8 ocho
9 nueve
10 diez

11 once
12 doce
13 trece
14 catorce
15 quince

16 dieciséis
17 diecisiete
18 dieciocho
19 diecinueve

20 veinte
21 veintiuno
22 veintidós
23 veintitrés
24 veinticuatro
25 veinticinco
26 veintiséis
27 veintisiete
28 veintiocho
29 veintinueve

30 treinta
31 treinta y uno
32 treinta y dos

40 cuarenta
41 cuarenta y uno
42 cuarenta y dos

50 cincuenta
51 cincuenta y uno
52 cincuenta y dos

60 sesenta
61 sesenta y uno
62 sesenta y dos

70 setenta
71 setenta y uno
72 setenta y dos

80 ochenta
81 ochenta y uno
82 ochenta y dos

90 noventa
91 noventa y uno
92 noventa y dos

100 cien (to)
200 doscientos
1.000 mil

Más vale pájaro en mano que ciento volando.

A bird in the hand is worth two in the bush.

Supplementary Vocabulary

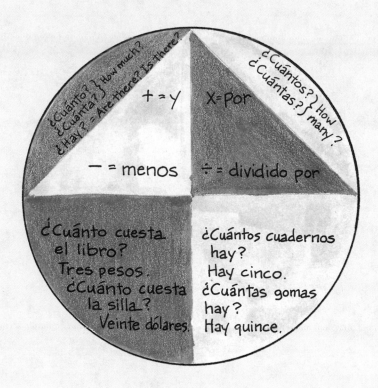

Exercises

A After you have studied the numbers and practiced saying them, try to write these numbers from memory. (En español, por favor.)

one _____ six _____

two _____ seven _____

three _____ eight _____

four _____ nine _____

five _____ ten _____

B Rate yourself. How did you do? Circle your evaluation.

1. very well 2. fairly well 3. poorly

C Practice again. Escribe los números.

EJEMPLO: __4__

1. cinco _____   4. nueve _____

2. ocho _____   5. siete _____

3. uno _____

D Escribe en español el nombre de cada número.

3 _____   6 _____

4 _____   10 _____

2 _____

E Tell whether the following equations indicate addition, subtraction, multiplication, or division.

1. Catorce dividido por siete son dos. _____

2. Dos y diez son doce. _____

3. Ocho por tres son veinticuatro. _____

4. Diecinueve menos trece son seis. _____

F Write the numbers in Spanish again and don't look at exercise A. (En español, por favor.)

1 _____   2 _____

6 _____   9 _____

8 _____   4 _____

3 _____   7 _____

5 _____   10 _____

¿Cuántos objetos hay en cada grupo? *How many objects are there in each group?*

 = _____

 = _____

 = _____

 = _____

 = _____

H ¿Cuántos objetos hay en total? *How many objects are there altogether?* _____

Now, write this sum in Spanish. _____

I Escribe las respuestas en español.

EJEMPLO: 6 − 4 = <u>dos</u>

1. 12 × 4 = _____

2. 30 − 10 = _____

3. 8 − 6 = _____

4. 12 + 18 = _____

5. 100 ÷ 2 = _____

6. 60 + 10 = _____

7. 30 − 15 = _____

8. 80 ÷ 2 = _____

9. 10 × 10 = _____

10. 15 + 4 = _____

J Your teacher will say ten numbers in Spanish. Write the corresponding numerals.

a. _____   f. _____

b. _____   g. _____

c. _____   h. _____

d. _____   i. _____

e. _____   j. _____

K How many interior angles are there in each figure? Circle the number.

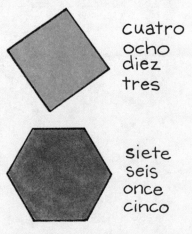

cuatro
ocho
diez
tres

siete
seis
once
cinco

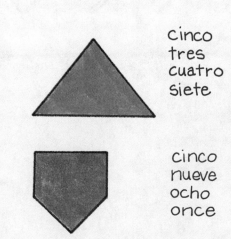

cinco
tres
cuatro
siete

cinco
nueve
ocho
once

L Lee el párrafo.

En la clase hay muchos objetos. Hay ocho gomas, veintitrés sillas, doce cuadernos y una papelera. Una goma cuesta treinta y cinco centavos y una silla cuesta diecisiete dólares. El cuaderno cuesta un dólar, veinticinco centavos y la papelera cuesta tres dólares.

Completa las frases.

1. En la clase hay. . . .
   a. tres objetos
   b. pocos objetos
   c. mil objetos
   d. muchos objetos

2. En total hay. . .objetos en la clase. (*Add.*)
   a. 4
   b. 44
   c. 25
   d. 13

Escoge la respuesta correcta.

3. ¿Cuánto cuesta una silla?
   a. 17 dólares
   b. 3 dólares
   c. 90 centavos
   d. 5 centavos

4. ¿Cuántas gomas hay en la clase?
   a. ocho
   b. ochenta
   c. dieciocho
   d. veintiocho

5. ¿Cuántas papeleras hay en la clase?
   a. once
   b. una
   c. muchas
   d. ochenta

Crucigrama

Vertical

1. $2 \times 3 =$
2. $4 + 4 =$
3. five dozens
5. a dozen plus one
7. Spanish for multiplication
8. how many
9. ½ century = ...years
11. $1 - 0 =$
12. five times twenty, plus one = ... *uno*

Horizontal

1. one hour and ten minutes = ...minutes
4. name of the sign indicating subtraction
5. $8 - 5 =$
6. one fewer than a dozen
9. $56 \div 4 =$
10. $50 - 10 =$
12. how much
13. $7 + 2 =$
14. the number of items in a pair
15. $70 - 40 =$
16. $80 + 8 =$

Teléfonos de Emergencia
Ciudad de México

Distrito Federal

Cruz Roja	557 5757
Cruz Verde	672 0606
Bomberos	768 3700
Seguro Social	211 0018
Policía y Tránsito	588 5100
Fugas de Gas	277 0422
Centro Antirrábico	549 4293
Policía de Caminos	684 2142
Cía. de Luz y Fuerza	546 4680
Locatel	658 1111
Escuadrón de Rescate	588 5100
Laser	551 6965
Rayo Azul	686 4038
Aristos	368 1212
Auxilio Turístico	250 8221

Ecatepec

Cruz Roja	787 1540
Bomberos	569 1444
Policía Municipal	787 3506

Naucalpan

Cruz Roja	576 3610
Antirrábico	576 9209
Policía Municipal	560 5210
Bomberos	373 1122

CANAL 44 DEPORTES

CANAL 48 INTERNACIONAL

CANAL 52 CLASICOS del cine TNT

CANAL 56 NOTICIAS

CANAL 60 CINE HBO Ole

CANAL 62 FAMILIAR

CANAL 64 INFANTIL

CANAL 50 CINE CANAL

CANAL 66 TELE UNO

UNO DE LOS DOS

1 ANIMALES

3 AUTOMOVILES

6 CONSTRUCCION

TVCABLE
BOGOTA

10 EMPLEOS

11 REPARACIONES

19 SECC. FIESTAS

21 RENTA CASAS

Geografía

 Poderoso caballero es don Dinero.   Money talks.

Important Cities

Madrid, the capital of Spain and its most populated city, is the geographical, artistic and cultural center of the nation.

Barcelona is Spain's largest seaport and its second largest city. It is the nation's most industrial city and is more cosmopolitan than Madrid.

Málaga—Spain's third largest city and the capital of the province of Andalucía—is a major Mediterranean seaport and Spain's summer playground.

Granada, the ancient capital of the Moorish empire, is a skiing center and site of the Alhambra, the palace of the ruling Moorish calif. The burial place of King Ferdinand and Queen Isabel is located in Granada's famous Gothic cathedral.

Sevilla is located on the Guadalquivir River and is the nation's largest inland port. It was once a center of Moorish culture and is still the site of the Giralda, a marvel of Moorish architecture.

Important Rivers

The *Ebro* is the only river in Spain that flows eastward. It empties into the Mediterranean.

The *Tajo* is Spain's longest river. It flows through Toledo, passes through Portugal and empties into the Atlantic at Lisbon.

The *Guadalquivir* is the most navigable river in Spain. It flows through Sevilla, its chief commercial port, and empties into the Atlantic.

The *Duero* drains north central and northwestern Spain. It flows west through Portugal to the Atlantic.

The *Guadiana* flows west from La Mancha to the border of Portugal. It then flows south to the Mediterranean.

> With the exception of the Guadalquivir, the rivers of Spain are for the most part unnavigable. They serve as a source of electric power and are used for pleasure boating. They are not used for shipping or transportation.

> Spain occupies the major part of the Iberian Peninsula and is almost completely surrounded by water. The sea plays a major role in the daily lives of many Spaniards.

MEXICO
Important Cities

México, D.F., is the capital and the business center of the country. With its 20,000,000 inhabitants it is the western hemisphere's most populated city and the cultural center of the nation.

Acapulco is a center of tourism and a popular beach resort on the Pacific Ocean.

Mérida, which lies southeast of the capital, is a site of Mayan architecture and culture.

Saltillo, located in the north central part of the country, enjoys a dry, comfortable climate. It is a university center of the nation.

Veracruz, a fishing center on the Gulf of Mexico, is famous for its distinctive cuisine and lively music.

Mexico is divided into two long vertical sections by a dual mountain chain called the *Sierra Madre*. This has served as a barrier to communication, transportation, and national unification. For those who can't afford to fly, travel through the Sierra Madre is long and difficult.

Important Facts

The Mayans and Aztecs built advanced civilizations long before the arrival of the Spanish.

Over eighty percent of Mexico's population is of Indian origin.

Mexico is the only Spanish-speaking nation in North America.

Mexico's foreign and domestic economy is based heavily on agriculture.

Lack of water is one of Mexico's greatest problems.

The *Río Bravo*—Mexican Spanish for *Río Grande*—forms part of the border between the United States and Mexico and flows into the Gulf of Mexico.

Exercises

A   Write the number of each city next to its name.

ESPAÑA

_____ Málaga

_____ Barcelona

_____ Granada

_____ Madrid

_____ Sevilla

MEXICO

_____ Veracruz

_____ Acapulco

_____ México, D.F.

_____ Mérida

_____ Saltillo

B   Name the cities suggested by the clues below.

1.   Spain's summer playground

_____

2.   most populated city of North America

_____

3.   site of the Alhambra

_____

4.   center of Mayan architecture

_____

5.   most cosmopolitan city of Spain

_____

6.   a university center in Mexico

_____

7.   port city on the Guadalquivir

_____

8.   fishing port on the Gulf of Mexico

_____

9.   capital and geographical center of Spain

_____

10. a Mexican resort city on the Pacific

_____

C   **Spain**. After studying the map carefully, find the following items.

1.   the river that flows from west to east   _____

2.   two rivers that flow through Portugal   _____

3.   the mountains dividing France and Spain   _____

4.   the country to the west of Spain   _____

5.   the river on which Sevilla is located   _____

D Match column **B** with column **A**.

A	B
1. Barcelona _____	a. Río Grande
2. Tajo _____	b. country to the west of Spain
3. Pirineos _____	c. Spain's northern port
4. Saltillo _____	d. city on the Guadalquivir
5. Sevilla _____	e. longest river in Spain
6. Río Bravo _____	f. Alhambra
7. Portugal _____	g. Mexican fishing resort
8. Veracruz _____	h. university city
9. Ebro _____	i. mountain boundary
10. Granada _____	j. flows eastward

E Escribe al lado del dibujo el nombre de la ciudad que pertenece. *Write the name of the city suggested by the picture.*

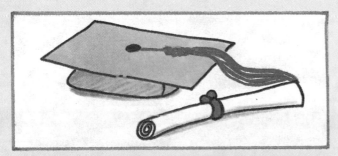

1. _____

2. _____

3. _____

4. _____

5. _____

F Escoge la palabra correcta. *Choose the correct word.*

1. *Sevilla* is a....
   a. river   b. mountain   c. country   d. city
2. Málaga is a port on the....
   a. Mediterranean   b. Atlantic   c. Pacific   d. Hudson
3. The Ebro flows to the....
   a. north   b. south   c. east   d. west
4. The *Pirineos* are....
   a. tribesmen   b. lakes   c. cities   d. mountains
5. The country to the west of Spain is....
   a. France   b. Portugal   c. Italy   d. Russia
6. Mérida is a city in....
   a. Cuba   b. Chile   c. Florida   d. Mexico
7. Toledo is a city on the....
   a. Duero   b. Ebro   c. Tajo   d. Guadiana
8. Saltillo is famous for its....
   a. salt   b. museums   c. fishing   d. universities
9. Veracruz is noted for its....
   a. food and music   b. politics   c. desert   d. churches
10. Granada was a...capital.
    a. Christian   b. Moorish   c. Roman   d. Portuguese

G Write in each blank space the answer that makes each statement geographically correct.

Spain is situated at the southwestern tip of Europe, just a short distance from the continent of Africa. 1.＿＿＿＿＿ (*city*), the 2.＿＿＿＿＿, is in the geographical center of the nation. Spain has 3.＿＿＿＿ (*number*) major rivers. The 4.＿＿＿＿ (*river*) is the only one that flows from 5.＿＿＿＿ to 6.＿＿＿＿. About two thirds of Spain's coast is bordered by the 7.＿＿＿＿＿＿＿＿＿＿ Sea. 8.＿＿＿＿＿＿＿＿＿＿ (*city*) in the northeast is the largest 9.＿＿＿＿ and Málaga in the 10.＿＿＿＿ is another major 11.＿＿＿＿. 12.＿＿＿＿＿ is an inland port located on the Guadalquivir. The 13.＿＿＿＿＿＿＿＿＿ mountains separate 14.＿＿＿＿＿ from 15.＿＿＿＿. They are found in the 16.＿＿＿＿＿＿＿＿＿ (*direction*) part of the country. 17.＿＿＿＿＿, a small country to the 18.＿＿＿＿, shares the Iberian Peninsula with Spain. The 19.＿＿＿＿＿＿＿＿＿ Sea forms the northwestern 20.＿＿＿＿＿ of Spain.

Projects

H

1. You are a tour guide hired to lead a group of scholars from the United States on a cultural and historical tour of Mexico. Name three cities you would show them and tell what they would see there.

2. Name three places you would like to visit if you were the winner of a three-week vacation in Spain during the winter recess. Tell why you would like to visit each place.

Maze

Marijosé and Miguel are ready to travel. Trace their vacation route to find out where they will be spending the summer. Name their destination in the space provided. List the places they will visit en route.

México, D.F.

Places they'll visit:

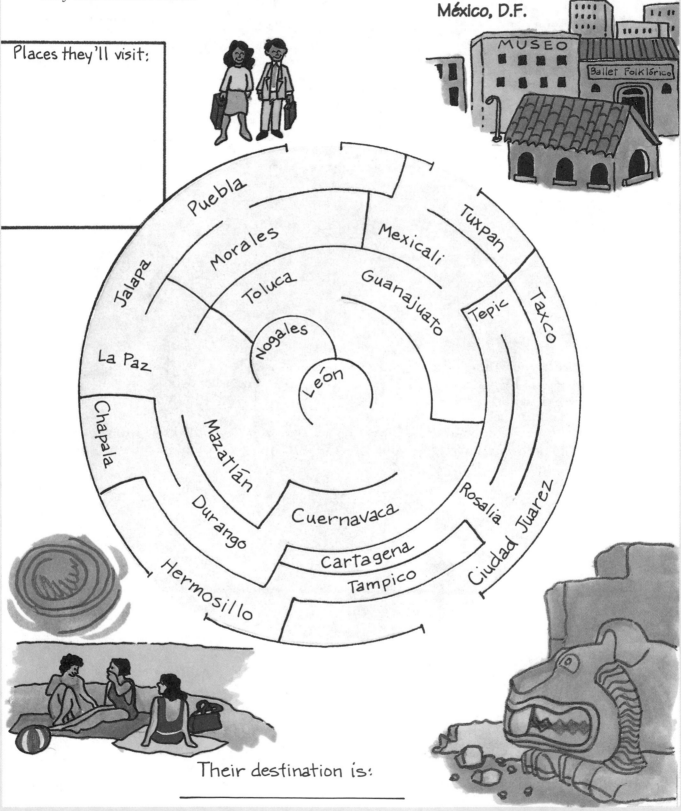

Their destination is:

_____

J

Vertical

1. site of Mayan ruins
3. Spain's inland port
4. home of the Alhambra
6. university city

Horizontal

1. country and capital with the same name
2. capital of Spain
5. Mexican city famous for music and food
7. Mexican resort on the Pacific
8. Spain's longest river
9. cosmopolitan city in Spain

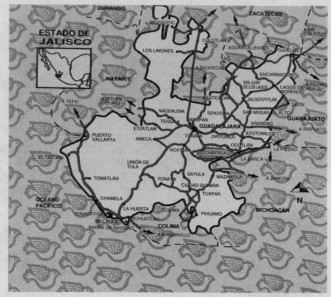

ESTADO DE JALISCO

N

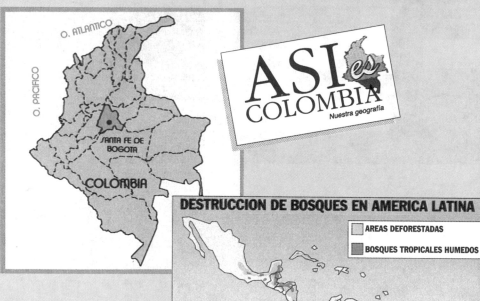

O. ATLANTICO

O. PACIFICO

SANTA FE DE BOGOTA

COLOMBIA

ASI es COLOMBIA

Nuestra geografía

DESTRUCCION DE BOSQUES EN AMERICA LATINA

☐ AREAS DEFORESTADAS

☐ BOSQUES TROPICALES HUMEDOS

PROMEDIO ANUAL

BRASIL	9.050.000
COLOMBIA	890.000*
MEXICO	615.000
ECUADOR	340.000
PERU	270.000
VENEZUELA	245.000
COSTA RICA	124.000
NICARAGUA	121.000
BOLIVIA	117.000
GUATEMALA	90.000
HONDURAS	90.000
PANAMA	36.000
EL SALVADOR	5.000
CUBA	2.000
JAMAICA	2.000
HAITI	2.000

* El IRM maneja una cifra superior que la calculada por el PAFC en Colombia.

Datos en hectáreas.
Fuente: Instituto de Recursos Mundiales

HOUSE
La casa

Clara: ¿Dónde vives?	Where do you live?
Beto: Vivo en una casa en Sevilla.	I live in a house in Seville.
José: ¿Dónde está el jardín?	Where is the garden?
Amanda: El jardín está allá.	The garden is over there.
Evita: ¿Dónde está el garaje?	Where is the garage?
Franco: Está detrás del jardín.	It's behind the garden.
Luz: ¿Cuántos cuartos hay en tu casa?	How many rooms are there in your house?
Carlos: Hay siete cuartos.	There are seven rooms.

Los cuartos de la casa

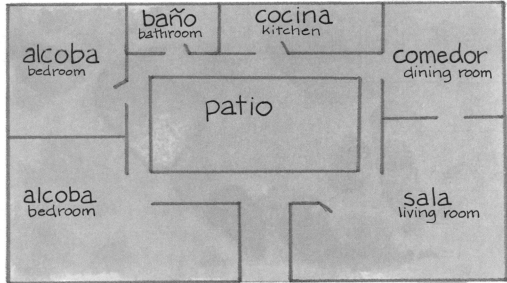

baño — bathroom	cocina — kitchen
alcoba — bedroom	comedor — dining room
patio	
alcoba — bedroom	sala — living room

 Cada oveja con su pareja.

Birds of a feather flock together.

1. mansión

2. casa particular

3. edificio de apartamentos

4. apartamento

5. remolque habitable

6. casucha

7. tienda de campaña

A Escribe el nombre de cada cuarto en español.

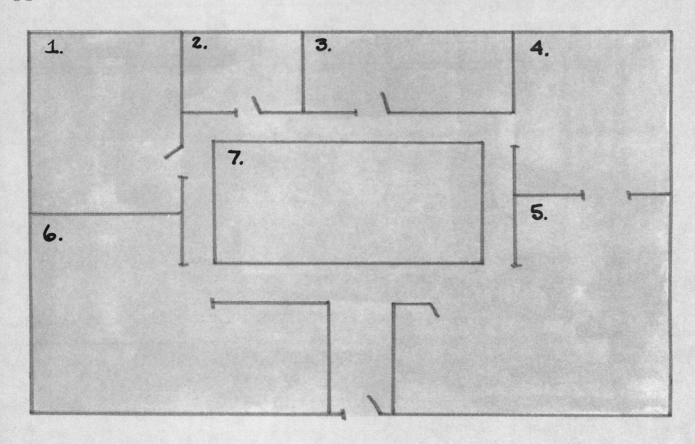

B Completa las frases.

1. Yo <u>cocino</u> en la _____.
        (cook)

2. Yo <u>duermo</u> en la _____.
        (sleep)

3. Yo <u>como</u> en el _____.
        (eat)

4. Yo <u>me baño</u> en el _____.
        (bathe)

5. Yo <u>juego</u> en el _____.
        (play)

6. Yo <u>descanso</u> en la _____.
        (relax)

C Escoge el nombre correcto para cada cuarto.

1. cocina   (bedroom   kitchen   bathroom)
2. sala   (living room   bedroom   kitchen)
3. comedor   (bedroom   bathroom   dining room)
4. alcoba   (dining room   bedroom   living room)
5. baño   (bedroom   kitchen   bathroom)

D In which room would you find a... (En español, por favor.)

1. bathtub? _____

2. dining table? _____

3. sofa? _____

4. stove? _____

5. nightstand? _____

E Completa cada frase en español.

1. A one-family house is called a _____.

2. A shack or hut is a _____.

3. When one goes camping, one sleeps in a _____.

4. A single unit in an apartment building is an _____.

5. A family on vacation might sleep in a _____.

6. A very wealthy family might live in a _____.

F Descifra las palabras.

1. INCOAC _____

2. ALAS _____

3. MOODREC _____

4. BACAOL _____

5. OPITA _____

CASA   FAMILIA   AMOR

G Lee el párrafo. Escoge las respuestas correctas.

Mi familia y yo vivimos en una casa bonita. La casa tiene seis cuartos. Hay flores en el patio. Quiero mucho a mi familia.

vivimos = we live	**tiene** = (it) has
hay = there is (are)	**quiero** = I love

1. Mi familia vive en....
   - a. un jardín
   - b. una casa
   - c. un cuarto
   - d. un patio

2. La casa es....
   - a. bonita
   - b. fea
   - c. grande
   - d. chica

3. La casa tiene...cuartos.
   - a. tres
   - b. nueve
   - c. seis
   - d. diez

4. El patio tiene....
   - a. cocina
   - b. baño
   - c. Madrid
   - d. flores

Crucigrama

H

Vertical

1. where the family eats
2. any room in a house
3. bedroom
5. living room
6. where the shower is
10. "...de campaña"

Horizontal

1. where food is prepared
4. poor family's shack
7. general word for house
8. flower garden, small yard
9. central open courtyard
11. "¿...vives?"
12. rich person's home

PLANTA BAJA

CAJON DE ESTACIONAMIENTO | ENTRADA | SALA | ESCALERA | 1/2 BAÑO | COMEDOR

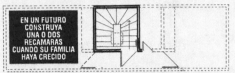

PLANTA ALTA

RECAMARA | ESCALERA | BAÑO | RECAMARA

EN UN FUTURO CONSTRUYA UNA O DOS RECAMARAS CUANDO SU FAMILIA HAYA CRECIDO

PLANTA ADICIONAL

FAMILY
La familia

Pablo: ¿Quién es?

Melinda: Es mi <u>hermano</u>.

Amanda: ¿Quiénes son?

Andrés: Son mis <u>nietos</u>.

Patricio: ¿Son tus <u>padres</u>?

Miguel: Sí, Ana es mi <u>madre</u> y Juan es mi <u>padre</u>.

Luz: Rosita, Paco y Clara son <u>hermanos</u>, ¿no?

Lorenzo: Sí, y también son mis <u>primos</u>.

Who is it?

It's my <u>brother</u>.

Who are they?

They're my <u>grandchildren</u>.

Are they your <u>parents</u>?

Yes, Ana is my <u>mother</u>, and Juan is my <u>father</u>

Rosita, Paco and Clara are <u>brother and sisters</u>, aren't they?

Yes, and they're also my <u>cousins</u>.

```
Recuerda:
Reunión familiar
Invitados
• abuelo, abuela
• mi tía Luisa y su esposo
• mi prima Sara
• mi primo Beto
• mi hermana y sus hijos
• Andrés y su esposa
• Marta y la nena
```

```
Remember:
Family Reunion
Guests
• grandfather, grandmother
• Aunt Luisa and her husband
• Cousin Sara
• Cousin Beto
• my sister and her children
• Andrés and his wife
• Marta and the baby (girl)
```

Andrés: ¿Dónde están tus <u>parientes</u>?

Cándida: Mis <u>abuelos</u> están adentro y mis <u>tíos</u> están en el jardín.

Guadalupe: ¿Están aquí tus <u>padrinos</u>?

Beto: ¡Cómo no! Mi <u>madrina</u> habla con mis <u>tías</u>. Mi <u>padrino</u> está en el patio.

Juanita: ¿Cómo se llaman tus <u>sobrinos</u>?

Franco: Mi <u>sobrino</u> es Pedro y mi <u>sobrina</u> es Lupe.

Juanita: ¿Eres tú su único <u>tío</u>?

Franco: No, Adán también es su tío.

Where are your <u>relatives</u>?

My <u>grandparents</u> are inside and my <u>aunts</u> and <u>uncles</u> are in the garden.

Are your <u>godparents</u> here?

Of course! My <u>godmother</u> is speaking with my <u>aunts</u>. My <u>godfather</u> is in the patio.

What are the names of your <u>nephew</u> and <u>niece</u>?

My <u>nephew</u> is Pedro, and my <u>niece</u> is Lupe.

Are you their only <u>uncle</u>?

No, Adán is their uncle as well.

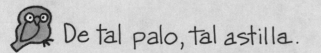 De tal palo, tal astilla.

A chip off the old block.

baby — el nene, la nena, la criatura

el niño (m.) child

la niña (f.) child

girl — la muchacha, la chica

la hija — daughter

el hijo — son

el muchacho, el chico — boy

la nieta — granddaughter

el nieto — grandson

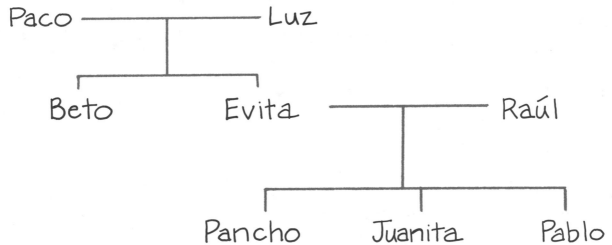

Paco ———————— Luz

Beto   Evita ———————— Raúl

Pancho   Juanita   Pablo

Exercises

A Indicate Juanita's relationship to each family member listed.

EXAMPLE

Juanita es la

1. _____ hermana _____ de Pancho.
2. _____ de Raúl.
3. _____ de Luz.
4. _____ de Beto.
5. _____ de Pablo.
6. _____ de Evita.
7. _____ de Paco.

B Haz lo mismo para Evita y Paco. *Do the same for Evita and Paco.*

Evita es la

1. _____ de Beto.
2. _____ de Raúl.
3. _____ de Pablo, Pancho
   y Juanita.
4. _____ de Luz y Paco.

Paco es el

1. _____ de Pablo, Pancho
   y Juanita.
2. _____ de Luz.
3. _____ de Beto y Evita.

C ¿Quién es...? *Who is...?* (En español, por favor.)

1. el hermano de mi padre

   Es mi _____.

2. la hija de mi tío

   Es mi _____.

3. la madre de mi madre

   Es mi _____.

4. el hijo de mi hermana

   Es mi _____.

5. la madre de mi hermano

   Es mi _____.

D Escoge la respuesta correcta.

1. ¿Dónde están los padres?
   a. on the bench
   b. in the playpen
   c. in the foreground

2. ¿Dónde está la nena?
   a. on the bench
   b. in the playpen
   c. in the foreground

3. ¿Dónde están los abuelos?
   a. on the bench
   b. in the playpen
   c. in the foreground

E ¿Quién soy yo? *Who am I?* (En español, por favor.)

1. I am your nephew's father. In other words, I am your _____.

2. I am your female sibling. In other words, I am your _____.

3. I am your sister's daughter. In other words, I am your _____.

4. I am your mother's father. In other words, I am your _____.

F Escribe en inglés.

1. ¿Quién es? _____

2. ¿Quién soy yo? _____

3. ¿Quién es la profesora? _____

4. ¿Quién prepara la lección? _____

G Completa en español.

1. ¿Quién es la chica?
   Ella es mi _____.
2. ¿Quién es el señor *(man)*?
   Es mi _____.
3. ¿Quién es el chico?
   Es mi _____.

H Lee el párrafo. Escribe el párrafo en inglés.

Mi familia

Mi familia es grande. Mi padre y mi madre tienen treinta y ocho años. Tengo dos hermanos y tres hermanas. Paco, mi hermano mayor, tiene dieciséis años. Mi hermanita Nilda tiene siete años. La familia vive en Santa Rosa.

vivir = to live	**tienen** = have
mayor = older	**tengo** = I have
-ito, -ita = (*diminutive suffix*) little	**tiene** = is (*when used with age*)

Tenemos muchísimos bebés

LA FAMILIA GRANDE VIAJA MEJOR...

Gracias a **Maeva** tu familia, por grande que sea, viaja mejor; porque aquí, tus DOS HIJOS MENORES DE 18 AÑOS, en All Inclusive NO PAGAN NADA. Y por si fuera poco, puedes traer acompañantes extras en la misma habitación ¡y ellos tendrán un descuento especial! ¿Lo ves? Hasta los amigos están bien incluidos en el Plan All Inclusive. No importa si tu familia es grande o pequeña, en Maeva viajan mejor.

MAEVA
ALL INCLUSIVE HOTELS & RESORTS
MEXICO
Manzanillo • Huatulco • Puerto Vallarta • Mayan Beach, Yucatán

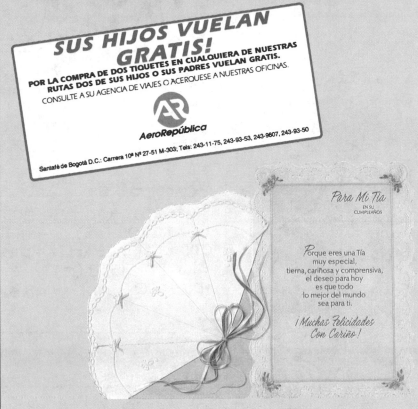

Para Mi Tía
EN SU
CUMPLEAÑOS

Porque eres una Tía
muy especial,
tierna, cariñosa y comprensiva,
el deseo para hoy
es que todo
lo mejor del mundo
sea para ti.

¡ Muchas Felicidades
Con Cariño !

POR SU FAMILIA

Cámbiese al Pollo!

Usted, cuida la salud de su familia, piensa en su futuro. El POLLO le da el balance perfecto para el bienestar en su hogar, ES SALUDABLE, ECONOMICO Y SABROSO.
Por todo esto...

EL ALIMENTO DE TODOS LOS DIAS

Feliz Cumpleaños,
HERMANA.

Profesiones y empleos

¿Cuál es tu profesión?
  Soy <u>actor</u>.
¿A qué te dedicas?
  Soy <u>actriz</u>.

What is your profession?
I am an <u>actor</u>.
What do you do (for a living)?
I am an <u>actress</u>.

artista   (m.&f.) = artist
cartero   (m.)   = mail carrier
comerciante (m.&f.)= businessperson
electricista (m.&f.)= electrician
músico   (m.)   = musician

Agencia de empleos Acme
  Buscamos un(a):

carpintero,-a   mecánico (m.)
cocinero,-a   médico,-a
enfermero,-a   plomero,-a
granjero,-a   profesor,-a

Empleo garantizado.

Tel.   12-59-43

Acme Employment Agency
  We are looking for:

carpenter   mechanic
cook   physician
nurse   plumber
farmer   teacher

Work guaranteed.

Tel. 12-59-43

El ejercicio hace maestro.   Practice makes perfect.

Exercises

A Number in order the professions or trades as the teacher recites them.

el médico _____   el cocinero _____

el mecánico _____   la comerciante _____

el cartero _____   el electricista _____

el enfermero _____   el granjero _____

B ¿Quién trabaja aquí? *Who works here?*

1. hospital _____

2. stage _____

3. school _____

4. wood shop _____

5. department store _____

6. restaurant _____

7. post office _____

8. garage _____

9. farm _____

10. studio _____

C Descifra las palabras.

1. LOPEROM _____

2. OTCAR _____

3. ITARTAS _____

4. TARCORE _____

5. TARZIC _____

D Write these sentences in English. Look first, then take a good guess.

1. Ana actúa en el teatro.

   _____

2. Mi tío repara autos.

   _____

3. Mi hermano es profesor.

   _____

4. El canta la música.

   _____

5. María estudia electricidad.

   _____

6. Papá es granjero.

   _____

7. Raúl prepara la comida.

   _____

E Guess who... (En español, por favor.)

1. El _____ instructs pupils.

2. La _____ administers to the sick.

3. La _____ paints portraits.

4. El _____ brings the mail.

5. El _____ wires the house for electric power.

6. El _____ repairs motors.

7. La _____ prepares food.

8. El _____ harvests the grain.

9. El _____ plays in a string quartet.

10. El _____ repairs broken pipes.

F Escribe en español la profesión o empleo que corresponde a cada dibujo.

1. _____

2. _____

3. _____

4. _____

5. _____

FELIZ DIA
DEL PILOTO

BOMBEROS

	119
Alarma	30 46 34
Comando	33 84 71
Información	36 43 77
Sub-estación	46 73 15
Provenza	
Sub-estación Chimitá	

POLICIA

D.A.S.	45 31 97
Estación Cien	33 90 15
SIJIN	33 68 29
Radio Patrulla	112

FOOD
La comida

¿Qué tenemos para comer?	What do we have to eat?
Tenemos ensalada.	We have salad.
¿Tienes hambre?	Are you hungry?
Sí, tengo hambre.	Yes, I'm hungry.
¿Tienes sed?	Are you thirsty?
No, no tengo sed.	No, I'm not thirsty.

Bodega de Patricio
Venta de bebidas

Café Caribe (½ kg)	30 pesos
Sangría El Pepe	45 pesos
Leche (un litro)	40 pesos
Chocolate Moctezuma	25 pesos
Agua mineral (2 litros)	40 pesos
Jugos Inca (lata)	35 pesos

Patrick's Grocery
Beverages

"Caribe" coffee ½ kg	30 pesos
"El Pepe" sangria	45 pesos
milk (1 liter)	40 pesos
Montezuma chocolate	25 pesos
Mineral water (2 liters)	40 pesos
Inca fruit juices (can)	35 pesos

El rincón de Juanita
comida típica

Menú del día —— Viernes

Desayuno especial
1. Continental con jugo natural 40 psts.
2. Campero
   Dos huevos, pan tostado,
   jamón o salchichas, papas
   Juanita, bebida   150 psts.

¡Calidad con sabor!

Joanie's Corner
regional food

Menu of the day —— Friday

Breakfast Special
1. "Continental" with fresh juice 40 psts.
2. "Farmer"
   Two eggs, toast, ham
   or sausage, Joanie's
   home fried potatoes,
   beverage   150 psts.
   Quality with taste!

 A buen hambre,
no hay pan duro.

To a hungry person there is
no hard bread.

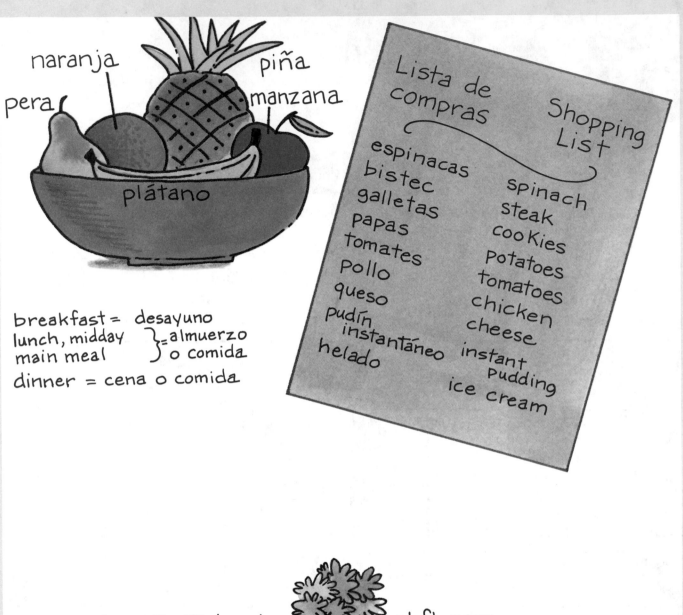

naranja

piña

pera

manzana

plátano

breakfast = desayuno
lunch, midday
main meal } = almuerzo o comida
dinner = cena o comida

Lista de compras

Shopping List

espinacas	spinach
bistec	steak
galletas	cookies
papas	potatoes
tomates	tomatoes
pollo	chicken
queso	cheese
pudín instantáneo	instant pudding
helado	ice cream

la pimienta
pepper

la sal
salt

el florero
vase

la taza
cup

la mantequilla
butter

el vaso
glass

el platillo
saucer

la servilleta
napkin

el plato
plate

el azúcar
sugar

el tenedor
fork

el cuchillo
knife

la cucharita
teaspoon

el mantel
table cloth

la cuchara
spoon

la mesa
table

58

Specialties of Spain and Latin America

Spain

Tortilla española—omelet laced with onions and diced potato, served hot as an entrée or eaten cold as a lunch

Paella valenciana—casserole of chicken and seafood served on a bed of saffron rice

Arroz con pollo—chicken and saffron rice served in a sauce seasoned with onion and garlic and cooked with fresh peas

Flan caramelo—custard served with a sauce of slightly burned sugar

Fresas con nata—fresh strawberries served with sweetened heavy whipped cream

Latin America

Ropa vieja (Cuba)—casserole containing ground beef, chicken, sausage, peppers, onions, and garlic in saffron rice

Chile con carne (Mexico)—ground beef, tomatoes, onion, green peppers, and kidney beans seasoned with chile powder

Churros—long doughnuts served with chocolate

Chocolate (Mexico)—thick hot chocolate often eaten with a spoon or used for dunking churros

Tacos (Mexico)—folded tortillas (corn flour pancakes) often filled with chile-flavored meat, refried beans, lettuce, tomatoes, cheese, and so on

> "¡Buen provecho!"—a wish on the part of a friend or host that all the guests may enjoy the meal and eat heartily

Exercises

A   Escribe el nombre de cada objeto en español.

1. _____

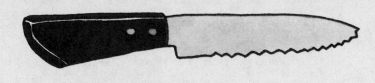

2. _____

3. _____

4. _____

5. _____

6. _____

B Completa cada frase en inglés.

1. A custard dessert quite popular in Spain is _____.

2. "Ropa vieja" is a casserole of assorted meats and vegetables originating in

   _____.

3. The two basic ingredients found in "arroz con pollo" are _____

   and _____.

4. A Mexican dish of ground beef, tomatoes, onions, green peppers, and kidney beans

   seasoned with chile powder is called _____.

5. "Ropa vieja," "tacos," and "chile con carne" are three popular foods in

   _____.

C Write three food items for each of the following categories.

meat	**vegetables**
1. _____	1. _____
2. _____	2. _____
3. _____	3. _____

dairy products	**beverages**
1. _____	1. _____
2. _____	2. _____
3. _____	3. _____

fruits	**desserts**
1. _____	1. _____
2. _____	2. _____
3. _____	3. _____

D **Projects**

Answer either 1 or 2 *and* 3 or 4.

1. You are opening a restaurant in Latin America. From your food list, prepare a menu for lunch and dinner. At least five dishes for each meal should be offered. Specialty dishes may be used.
2. Prepare a poster from magazine pictures. Show a balanced breakfast and a balanced dinner. Label each food item with its Spanish name.
3. Prepare fifteen different flashcards each with a picture of a food item on one side and its Spanish name on the other.
4. In Spanish, list fifteen words that name foods. Then scramble each word. These can be used in classroom games. Examples: LECHE = EHLCE / CAFE = AFCE

Crucigrama

E

Vertical

1. enjoyed with chocolate
2. where tacos originated
3. Mexican beef-vegetable dish
4. Spanish chicken casserole
5. sauce served over flan
6. meat- and vegetable-filled corn cakes
8. popular Spanish dessert

Horizontal

1. beverage from Mexico
6. Spanish word for omelet
7. Cuban casserole
9. where paella and flan are popular
10. what is set for meals
11. served over "fresas"
12. country of origin, "ropa vieja"
13. dinnertime wish

Jugosas Frescas Sabrosas

Naturalmente

Las más jugosas, frescas y sabrosas frutas son de *FRUTASA*, esencia de nuestra tierra.

Provienen de cultivos propios altamente tecnificados controlados por agrónomos especializados para garantizar su gran calidad.

Por eso, cuando usted desee comprar frutas busque el SELLO *FRUTASA*, garantía de calidad y frescura.

FRUTASA

da sabor a tu vida

ESPECIALES del Día

DESAYUNOS

(DE 7:00 AM a 12:00 PM)

JUGO O FRUTA
CAFÉ, TE O LECHE
HUEVOS CHIAPANECOS
Huevos revueltos con jamón y tortilla dorada bañados con salsa verde y gratinados con queso Chihuahua, servidos con frijoles charros.
N$ 16.00

MOLLETES CON CHORIZO
Ricos bolillos rellenos de frijoles refritos con chorizo y gratinados con queso, servidos con salsa mexicana. N$ 13.50

HUEVOS A LA FLORENTINA
Huevos estrellados montados sobre cama de espinacas, bañados con salsa blanca y gratinados con queso Chihuahua.
N$ 15.00

PAN TOSTADO O TORTILLAS

COMIDAS

CREMA ARGENTIU
o
CONSOME DE POLLO
o
COCTEL DE FRUTAS

HIGADO DE RES ENCEBOLLADO
Sabroso hígado de res encebollado servido con puré de papa. N$ 24.00

MANCHA MANTELES
Picosito guiso con lomo de cerdo y pollo servido con frutas y almendras acompañado de arroz blanco.
N$ 26.00

LENGUA DE RES A LA MOSTAZA
Deliciosa lengua de res guisada con salsa de mostaza, acompañada de puré de papa.
N$ 25.50

POSTRE A ELEGIR
Gelatina, nieve o helado.

BEBIDAS
Café, té o refresco.
Pan y mantequilla.

S4L

Bien mexicana y muy natural

Salsa Casera
MEXICANA PICANTE
Con todo Confianza... es
HERDEZ.
CONTENIDO NETO: 210 g

POSTRES

Helado cremoso de chocolate

¿Cuál es la receta?

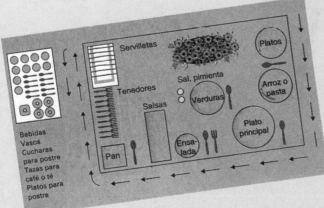

Bebidas
Vasos
Cucharas
para postre
Tazas para
café o té
Platos para
postre

Pan

Salsas

Tenedores

Servilletas

Sal, pimienta

Verduras

Ensa-
lada

Plato
principal

Arroz o
pasta

Platos

CRIOLLA A LA OLLA

La papa criolla tiene fósforo, proteínas, fibra, calcio, vitaminas A y B y muchas maneras ricas de prepararla.

CONSULTE
A FEDEPAPA

ART
El arte

10

Three Great Artists

El Greco, Doménikos Theotokópoulos (1541–1614), was born on the isle of Crete. He studied art in Venice, Italy, before going to Spain in 1577. He settled in Toledo under the sponsorship of the governor, for whom he painted many religious works. The artistic style used by El Greco has been called realistic mysticism, an art style that began in Spain with him. It is characterized by the elongated and delicate traits of the human body. The good people look as if they could almost float to heaven. A simple formula for this style is: *light and delicate: good = darkness and bulk: evil.* The *Burial of the Count of Orgaz* is one of El Greco's masterpieces.

Diego Velázquez (1599–1660) is the father of Spanish realism. His successful career began at the age of twenty when he painted *The Water Carrier of Seville.* Several years later he was appointed royal court artist, a position he held until his death. Velázquez is famous for the way he painted the people and objects around him. He made them look real. He treated noblemen, tradesmen, and peasants with dignity and respect. By using color and light skillfully, he gave life and feeling to all his paintings. Velázquez is the greatest Spanish artist of the classical era.

Francisco de Goya was born near Zaragoza. He went to Madrid at twenty-seven and soon became famous as a master of two styles of art, the rococo and the neobaroque.

Goya painted the social customs of Spanish peasant life. He also painted the royal court and the innocent victims of the Napoleonic forces of France. Later in life, Goya became depressed by the world around him and began to paint people and things in a distorted and ugly way. Discouraged by the cruelty around him, he went to France, where he died in 1828. *The Parasol* is one of his best paintings.

A caballo regalado no se le mira el diente.

Never look a gift horse in the mouth.

The Burial of the Count of Orgaz
(oil on canvas, 1586)
by El Greco
Catedral de Santo Tomás, Toledo, Spain

The Water Carrier of Seville
(oil on canvas, 1619–20)
by Diego Velázquez
Victoria and Albert Museum, London

Don Manuel Osorio de Zúñiga
(oil on canvas, 1788)
by Francisco de Goya
The Metropolitan Museum of Art, New York

The Parasol
(oil on canvas, 1777)
by Francisco de Goya
Museo del Prado, Madrid

Exercises

A Name the picture that shows:

1. a man selling water. _____

2. a nobleman being buried in the church. _____

3. a young prince at play. _____

B Name the Spanish artist whose works reveal:

1. light and darkness as symbols. _____

2. realistic portrayal of the human body. _____

3. pastoral scenes. _____

4. a spiritualized human form. _____

5. lighting and color reflecting reality. _____

6. people and things painted in a distorted manner. _____

C Asocia la frase en inglés con el nombre en español.

A	B
1. Toledo _____	a. mystical painting
2. Goya _____	b. father of Spanish realism
3. Velázquez _____	c. Doménikos Theotokópoulos
4. El Greco _____	d. home of El Greco
5. *The Burial of the Count of Orgaz* _____	e. painter of rural life

D Complete the analogies.

1. Madrid: Velázquez = Toledo: _____

2. country life: _____ = court life: Velázquez

3. Velázquez: realism = El Greco: _____

4. governor: El Greco = _____ : Velázquez

¿Qué nombre corresponde al dibujo?

El Greco

Velázquez

Goya

F Which artist would most likely be...

1. attending an elaborate church ceremony? _____

2. using a live horse for exact proportion? _____

3. painting peasants at work and play? _____

G In your opinion...

1. whose paintings could decorate a Gothic cathedral?

   _____

2. whose paintings show things as they really are?

   _____

3. whose paintings show how poor country people live?

   _____

H Which of the paintings in this unit do you like best? _____

Who created this masterpiece? _____

State in your own words what the picture is about and why you like it.

_____

_____

_____

_____

_____

I Escribe las palabras que faltan.

1. Diego _____ worked in the Royal Palace in

   _____.

2. El Greco was sponsored by the _____ of

   _____.

3. Francisco _____ was born in Zaragoza and worked in

   _____.

GALERIA PIRAMIDE

Los mejores pintores

Fernando Oramas
Grau
Iván Loboguerrero
Pablo Angarita
Lázaro Hernández
María Clara Trujillo
Hermes Pinto
Alejandro Spinosa
Fernando Vásquez
Néstor Plazas
Hernando Carrero

**Dibujos - óleos
Artistas contemporáneos
Arte Primitivo colombiano**

MUSEO DEL ORO

BANCO DE LA REPUBLICA

MUSEOS		
		Tel.282 07 60
	Cra 6 # 7-43	Tel.286 04 66
MUSEO ARQUEOLOGICO	Cll 26 # 6-05	Tel.246 36 06
MUSEO DE ARTE MODERNO	Cra 15 # 0-56s	Tel.342 12 66
MUSEO DE ARTES GRAFICAS	Cra 8 # 7-21	Tel.241 60 17
MUSEO DE ARTES Y TRAD. POP.	Cra 6 # 9-77	Tel.283 63 09
MUSEO DE ARTE COLONIAL	Cll 26 cra 7	
MUSEO DE HIST. NATURAL		Tel.225 90 58
(PLANETARIO DISTRITAL)		Tel.342 77 77
MUSEO DE CIENCIAS	Cra 48# 63-97	Tel.616 37 91
MUSEO DEL ORO	Cll 16 # 5-41	Tel.289 62 75
MUSEO DEL CHICO	Cra 7 # 93-01	Tel.258 22 50
MUSEO FCO JOSE DE CALDAS	Cra 8 # 6-87	Tel.222 03 23
MUSEO F.J.DE P. SANTANDER	Cra 7 # 150-01	Tel.281 31 31
MUSEO. G.N. DE INGEOMINAS	Dg. 53 # 34-53	Tel.342 59 25
MUSEO MILITAR	Cll 10 # 28-66	Tel.203 00 25
MUSEO NACIONAL	Cra 7 # 28-66	Tel.281 75 05
MUSEO NARIÑO	Cra 38 # 10-29s	
MUSEO DEL SIGLO XIX	Cra 8 # 7-93	Tel.334 41 50
(Fdo. Cult. Cafetero)		Tel.284 68 19
MUSEO 20 DE JULIO	Cll 11 # 6-94	
MUSEO QUINTA DE BOLIVAR	Cll 20 # 3-23e	

Joan Miró

PARTS OF THE BODY
Las partes del cuerpo

la cabeza

el cuello

el hombro

el codo

el pecho

el brazo

el estómago

la mano

la pierna

la rodilla

el pie

Una mano lava la otra.　　　One hand washes the other.

el pelo

la frente

la oreja

la boca

los labios

el ojo

la nariz

los dientes

la barbilla

Las partes de la cara
parts of the face

el dedo = the finger
el dedo (del pie) = the toe
el diente = the tooth
el labio = the lip

A Label the parts of the body. (En español, por favor.)

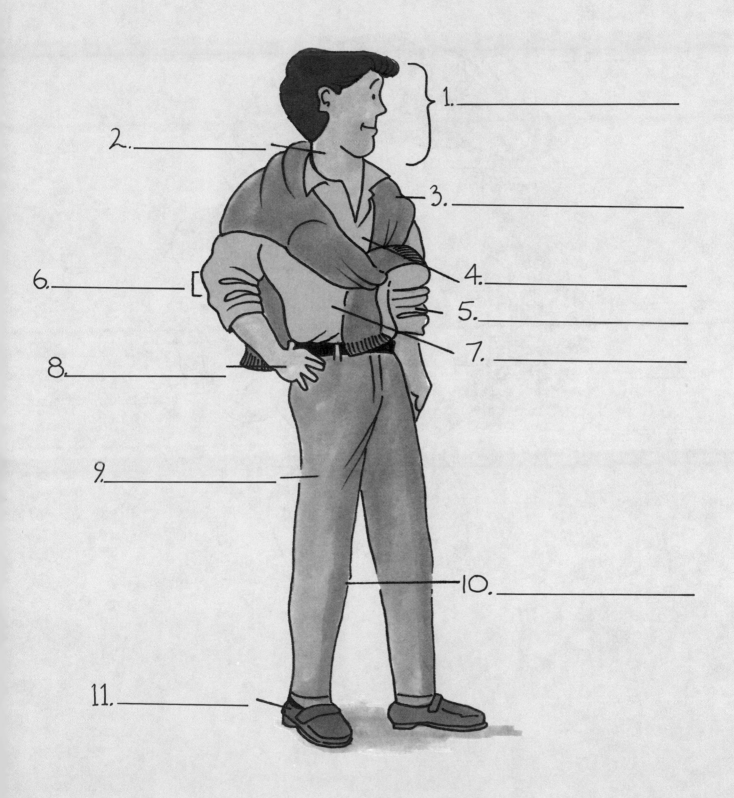

1. _____

2. _____

3. _____

4. _____

5. _____

6. _____

7. _____

8. _____

9. _____

10. _____

11. _____

B Label the parts of the face. (En español, por favor.)

1.————————

2.————————

3.————————

4.——————

5.————

6.——————

7.————————

8.——————————

9.————————

C Complete the analogies.

1. la rodilla: la pierna = _____ : el brazo

2. _____ : el pie = el brazo: la pierna

3. los dedos: _____ = los dedos del pie: el pie

4. los labios: la boca = el pelo: _____

D Completa cada frase en español.

1. We see with our _____ .

2. The tongue is in the _____ .

3. The _____ helps us listen.

4. The pen is held in the _____ .

5. The _____ are needed to chew food.

6. The toes are found on the _____ .

7. We use the _____ to smell a rose.

8. We play a guitar with our _____ .

9. The "funny bone" is located on the _____ .

10. Digestion takes place chiefly in the _____ .

E Guess the meaning of the underlined verbs.

1. Yo <u>hablo</u> con la boca. _____

2. Yo <u>toco</u> con el dedo. _____

3. Yo <u>veo</u> con el ojo. _____

4. Yo <u>oigo</u> con la oreja. _____

5. Yo <u>huelo</u> con la nariz. _____

F Name the part of the body associated with each illustration. (En español, por favor.)

1. _____

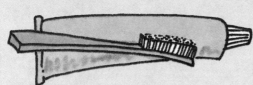

2. _____

3. _____

¡Qué idea!

4. _____

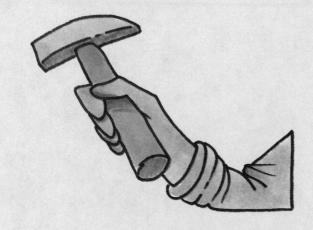

5. _____

6. _____

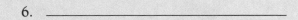

7. _____

8. _____

9. _____

10. _____

G Asocia la palabra en inglés con la palabra en español. (*Match the activity in column* **B** *with the Spanish word in column* **A**.)

A	B
1. mano _____	a. kneeling
2. ojos _____	b. smelling
3. orejas _____	c. thinking
4. boca _____	d. speaking
5. cabeza _____	e. walking
6. dedos _____	f. writing
7. brazo _____	g. listening
8. rodillas _____	h. touching
9. nariz _____	i. seeing
10. pies _____	j. carrying

H Lee el párrafo. Escoge las respuestas correctas.

Mi cuerpo es una máquina fantástica. Tengo dos orejas, dos ojos, dos labios, dos brazos, dos manos, dos piernas y dos pies. Tengo una cabeza, una nariz y una lengua. Mi cuerpo tiene veinte dedos y treinta y dos dientes. Mi cabeza controla mi cuerpo. Mi cuerpo es maravilloso, ¿no?

máquina = machine

1. Mi cuerpo es. . . .
   a. un animal
   c. una institución
   b. una máquina
   d. un desastre

2. Tengo dos. . . .
   a. brazos
   c. dientes
   b. cabezas
   d. lenguas

3. Mi cuerpo tiene más (*more*) de diez. . . .
   a. narices
   c. ojos
   b. pies
   d. dientes

4. Mi cabeza controla mi. . . .
   a. nariz
   c. cuerpo
   b. pies
   d. lengua

5. Mi cuerpo es. . . .
   a. enorme
   c. pobre
   b. fantástico
   d. elegante

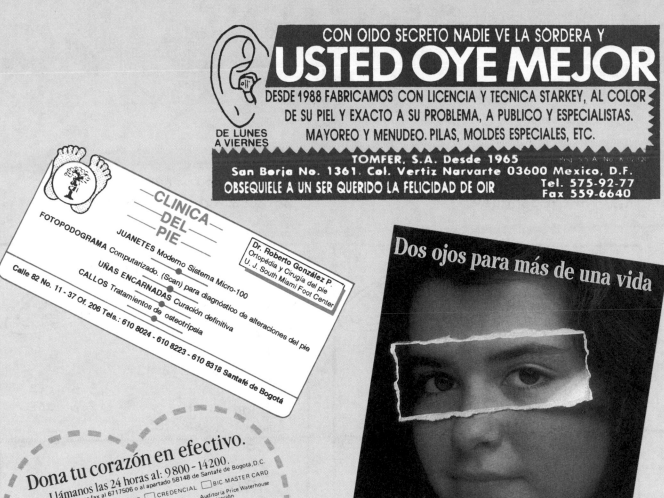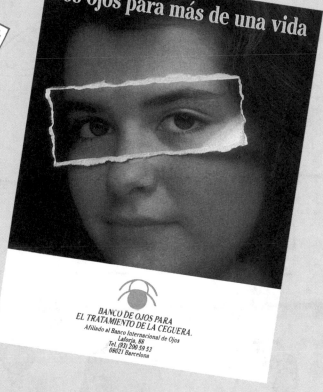

CLOTHING
La ropa

¿Qué llevas ?
Llevo mi ropa nueva.

What are you wearing?
I am wearing my new clothes.

Lini
Vacaciones de invierno
Chile — julio

2 vestidos de lana
3 sombreros
3 pares de pijamas
2 cinturones   3 camisas
12 pañuelos   2 blusas
2 suéteres de lana
   calcetines   abrigo
   guantes
   pantalones
   zapatos

Lini
Winter Vacation
Chile — July

2 woolen dresses
3 hats
3 pairs of pajamas
2 belts   3 shirts
12 handkerchiefs   2 blouses
2 woolen sweaters
   socks   overcoat
   gloves
   pants
   shoes

Modas de Susana
ropa exterior e interior

blusa

vestido

falda

zapatillas

corbata

chaqueta

camisa

bata

traje

Ayer ranchero, hoy caballero.

Clothes make the man.

Exercises

A Asocia la palabra en inglés con la palabra en español.

	A		**B**
1.	abrigo _____	a.	skirt
2.	pañuelo _____	b.	suit
3.	chaqueta _____	c.	sweater
4.	sombrero _____	d.	bathrobe
5.	falda _____	e.	dress
6.	traje _____	f.	handkerchief
7.	zapatos _____	g.	jacket
8.	vestido _____	h.	hat
9.	bata _____	i.	overcoat
10.	suéter _____	j.	shoes

B What do you wear...(En español, por favor.)

1. to a symphony? _____

2. to bed? _____

3. to school? _____

4. in cold weather? _____

5. in cool weather? _____

C Complete the analogies.

1. guantes: manos = _____ : pies

2. _____ : falda = camisa: pantalones

3. corbata: camisa = _____ : pantalones

D   ¿Qué llevas?

1. Llevo un _____.

2. Llevo un _____.

3. Llevo una _____.

4. Llevo una _____

    y una _____.

5. Llevo una _____

    y una _____.

E Escribe las palabras en inglés.

1. llevar _____

2. lleva _____

3. llevo _____

4. llevas _____

F Completa en inglés.

1. An "abrigo" goes (under / over) _____ a suit coat.

2. A "blusa" is worn with a _____.

3. A "cinturón" is worn on one's _____.

4. The "zapatos" are worn on the _____.

5. A "corbata" is worn with a _____.

G List the required number of items for each category. (En español, por favor.)

outerwear (5)   **accessories (3)**

_____   _____

_____   _____

_____   _____

_____

_____

footwear (3)   **sleepwear (1)**

_____   _____

_____

_____

H Lee el párrafo. Escoge las respuestas correctas.

Esta noche yo asisto al concierto de música clásica con mis padres. Llevo un traje nuevo, una camisa y una corbata. Como hace frío, llevo un abrigo sobre mi ropa nueva. Llevo también los guantes nuevos.

> **tiempo** = weather
> **Hace frío.** = It's cold.

1. ¿A qué función asisto yo esta noche?
   a. una función musical
   b. un circo
   c. una clase de inglés

2. ¿Qué llevo?
   a. una blusa
   b. una sonrisa
   c. un traje

3. ¿Qué tiempo hace?
   a. frío
   b. calor
   c. buen tiempo

4. ¿Qué llevo sobre mi ropa?
   a. ropa interior
   b. un abrigo
   c. un vestido

Crucigrama

Vertical

2. worn over a coat
3. sleepwear
4. worn when a jacket is too warm
5. often worn with a skirt
9. pants, jacket, and vest of the same color
11. hat
12. often worn with a blouse
14. includes all articles of clothing
15. worn over nightwear

Horizontal

1. feet protectors
6. secures pants
7. hand warmers
8. woman's outer garment
10. trousers
13. short hosiery
16. indoor footwear
17. neckwear
18. handkerchief

Zapato casual **California**, tallas 22 a la 25, en colores de moda. De N$32.

NS **19**⁸⁰

Unicentro Bogotá *Unicentro Cali* *Galerías Bogotá*

Ropa ★★★★★ **Damas**

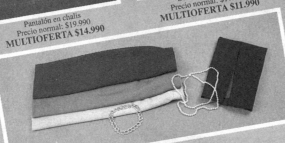

Blusa unicolor en chalis, manga larga
Precio Normal: $17.950
MULTIOFERTA $13.950

Pantalón en chalis
Precio normal: $19.990
MULTIOFERTA $14.990

Bermuda en chalis
Precio normal: $17.990
MULTIOFERTA $11.990

Falda en lino larga
Precio Normal: $19.990
MULTIOFERTA $13.990

Casa Grajales ⊛ *Siempre su Hogar !*

TRAFFIC...¡FRESCA MODA!
Camisas manga corta, lisa, 2 bolsas, 100% alg. Tallas: Ch, M, G.
A SOLO N$89.00

TIME
AND COLORS
La hora y los colores

¿Qué hora es?   What time is it?

Es la una y media.

Son las diez
menos cuarto.

Son las tres.

Es mediodía.

¿A qué hora?   At what time...?

A las siete y cuarto.   A medianoche.

A las dos y cinco.

A las doce menos
cinco.

"Es" is used with "la una," "mediodía," and "medianoche."
Transportation in Europe operates on official time, which is on a
twenty-four hour basis. Official time is often used by
schools, radio and television stations, theaters and movie
theaters.

 Más vale tarde que nunca.   Better late than never.

¿De qué color es...?   What color is...?
   Es...   It is...
¿De qué color son...?   What color are...?
   Son...   They are...

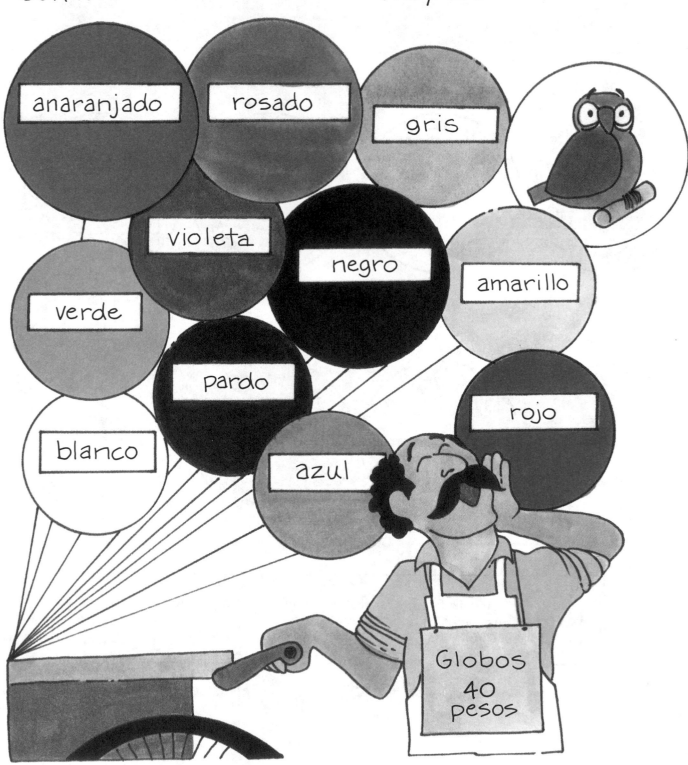

anaranjado

rosado

gris

violeta

negro

amarillo

verde

Pardo

rojo

blanco

azul

Globos
40
pesos

Exercises

A Listen as your teacher indicates a time. Find the clock that shows that time, and label it number 1. Then your teacher will express another time. Mark the clock expressing that time number 2. Continue until all eight clocks are numbered.

B Completa cada frase en español.

1. The colors of the American flag are _____, _____, and _____.

2. In spring the grass is very _____.

3. When the weather is pleasant, the sky is azure or _____.

4. A shade produced by mixing "negro" and "blanco" is _____.

5. Lemons and dandelions are _____.

6. Flour is _____.

7. Tar is _____.

8. A carrot is _____.

9. Chocolate icing is _____.

10. A color attained by blending "rojo" and "blanco" is _____.

C Escribe en español.

1. at one o'clock _____

2. It's half past four. _____

3. at 5:25 _____

4. It's 7:45. _____

5. at a quarter after nine _____

D Asocia el español con el inglés.

1. milk or snow _____   a. verde

2. a strawberry _____   b. azul

3. tar or a tire _____   c. blanco

4. a forget-me-not or a robin's egg _____   d. rojo

5. spinach _____   e. negro

E Lee el párrafo. Escoge las respuestas correctas.

Paco García va al cine con su amiga Marisela. La película comienza a las ocho. Paco va a llevar su nuevo traje azul, una camisa blanca y una corbata roja. Marisela va a llevar su blusa amarilla con calcetines amarillos y una nueva falda verde. Los dos llevan zapatos negros. Son las seis y media de la tarde y Paco va a la casa de Marisela.

> **va** = he / she goes   **va a llevar** = is going to wear
> **van** = they go   **película** = film

1. La amiga de Paco es...
   a. su madre.   b. Raúl.
   c. su hermana.   d. Marisela.

2. Paco y Marisela van al...
   a. museo.   b. teatro.
   c. parque.   d. cine.

3. La corbata de Paco es...
   a. verde.   b. roja.
   c. azul.   d. blanca.

4. Los calcetines de Marisela son...
   a. amarillos.   b. rojos.
   c. negros.   d. grises.

5. Paco va a la casa de Marisela...
   a. a las 7:15.   b. a las 6:45.
   c. a las 6:30.   d. a las 8:00.

Son las 9:00.

F Color the clock according to the directions.

1. Color the "pies" ROJO.
2. Color the "cara" PARDO.
3. Color the "dientes" AZUL.
4. Color the "ojos" VERDE.
5. Color the "pelo" BLANCO.
6. Color the "nariz" ROJO.
7. Color the "siete" GRIS.
8. Color the "dos" ANARANJADO.
9. Color the "ceros" VIOLETA.
10. Color the "nueve" ROSADO.
11. Color the "uno" NEGRO.
12. Color the "tres." AMARILLO.

MUSIC
La música

Three Great Musicians

Antonio Soler (1729–83), a contemporary of Bach and Vivaldi's, is Spain's foremost baroque musician. His music displays the movement, vigor, and counterpoint that are the characteristics of the baroque style.

Like Vivaldi, he was both a priest and a composer. His organ compositions were created almost exclusively for church functions.

Like Bach, he was an expert on both the organ and the harpsichord. Several of his superb sonatas for the harpsichord are still performed by many modern symphony orchestras. Soler, like Bach, was an expert on organ construction. His suggestions were employed in constructing organs for several European cathedrals. His most noted works are entitled *Sonatas for the Harpsichord.*

Juan Crisóstomo Arriaga (1806–26) is the father of the classical movement in Spain and its most celebrated composer. He is called the "Spanish Mozart" because his short life, his musical style, and his great achievements parallel the life of Mozart. Arriaga wrote his first opera at the age of twelve without the help of formal training in harmony. At that same age he began violin studies and at sixteen was recognized as a virtuoso. In 1823 he studied music in Paris and was recognized as a genius.

Arriaga wrote an opera, a symphony, chamber music and church music. His most famous works include *Symphony in D*, *Quartets for Strings*, and Spain's most famous piece of church music, *Et vitam venturi.*

Manuel de Falla (1876–1946) was born in Cádiz. He studied music at the National Conservatory of Madrid. In 1905 his opera *La vida breve* earned him his nation's highest honor. This musical genius incorporated popular music into almost all the classical forms. His operas, ballets, and concertos are precise and lively. The music of de Falla has wide appeal because of its use of the popular music of his time. *La vida breve*, *El sombrero de tres picos*, and *Fantasía bética* are three of his compositions. Manuel de Falla was a contemporary of Maurice Ravel, Aaron Copland, and Samuel Barber's.

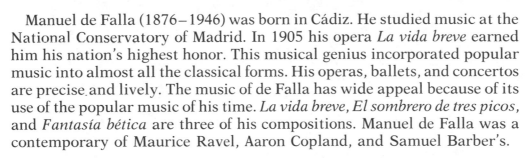

El que canta, sus males espanta.   Singing frightens troubles away.

Exercises

A Give the full name and the dates of the composer who...

1. used popular music in his compositions. _____

2. wrote music for the harpsichord and built organs. _____

3. was a boy genius and expert violinist. _____

B Asocia columna **B** con columna **A**.

A		**B**
1. Juan Arriaga _____		a. baroque harpsichordist
2. *Et vitam venturi* _____		b. used popular themes in classical forms
3. Antonio Soler _____		c. "Spanish Mozart"
4. *El sombrero de tres picos* _____		d. Spanish church music
5. Manuel de Falla _____		e. a famous ballet

C Guess who was...

1. a violin virtuoso? _____

2. a teacher of the organ? _____

3. an expert on organ construction? _____

4. a composer of ballet music? _____

5. the writer of a famous church song? _____

D Complete the analogies.

1. Soler: organ = _____: violin

2. *Et vitam venturi*: Arriaga = *El sombrero de tres picos*: _____

3. _____: baroque music = De Falla: modern music

4. Soler: Bach = Arriaga: _____

5. _____: Soler = Manuel: De Falla

E Add the names of Soler, Arriaga, and De Falla to the lists of their contemporaries.

1. Mozart, Haydn, Cherubini _____

2. Bach, Vivaldi, Handel _____

3. Ravel, Copland, Barber _____

F ¿Qué nombre corresponde a cada dibujo?

Arriaga

Soler

De Falla

G Descifra las palabras.

1. NOOTINA _____

2. AJNU _____

3. ULEMNA _____

4. LORES _____

5. AFLALED _____

Crucigrama

H

Vertical

1. contemporary of Bach and Vivaldi's
2. birthplace of modern composer
4. *Et* _____ *venturi,* church music by Arriaga
5. *El sombrero de tres picos*
6. the "Spanish Mozart"

Horizontal

2. place where Soler's music was performed
3. nationally acclaimed opera
7. first name of Spanish baroque musician
8. first name of violin virtuoso

▲ ORC

Stereo **97.7 FM** La Estación

BAÑATE EN MUSICA

MARIACHI
LOS HALCONES
DE MEXICO

SERENATAS - REUNIONES SOCIALES
DIA
45 28 49 - 33 56 01
33 32 56 - 40 10 18
33 12 61 - 33 69 58
NOCHE INFORMA JUAN PIMIENTO

Maná ¡NUESTRA
MUSICA
ES MUY
CALIENTE!

LA ONDA

Vaselina

LA BANDA
ROCK

Disponible en Compact Disc y Cassette

Pónganse botas, quítense tenis

MELODY

TOTALMENTE HABLADA Y CANTADA EN ESPAÑOL
BASADA EN LA PRODUCCION ORIGINAL DE LONDRES

El FANTASMA de la OPERA

COMEDIA MUSICAL
de KEN HILL

Música de
Verdi, Gounod,
Offenbach,
Mozart, Weber
y Donizetti

DEL 11 AL 22 DE AGOSTO

Boletos a la venta a partir del
Martes 3 de Agosto

Venta de Boletos en el Sistema TICKETMASTER

● Taquillas del **Teatro de los Insurgentes.**
● Centros Tiendas Mixup: Plaza Lindavista, Zona Rosa,
Centro Coyoacán, Plaza Universidad, Perisur, Galerías Coapa, Galerías
Insurgentes y Pabellón Polanco. Tiendas Discolandia: Plaza Tepeyac,
Metro Ermita, San Cosme, Tlalnepantla, Teatros Lomas
Verdes, Auditorio Nacional, Palacio de los Deportes
y Gimnasio Juan de la Barrera.
Ahora también en tiendas Gran Bazar: Tepeyac y Lomas.
● Centro Telefónico ☎ 325.9000

ti
teatro de los
insurgentes

HORARIOS
1a. SEMANA

MIER.11	8:30 P.M.
JUEV.12	8:30 P.M.
VIER. 13	9:00 P.M.
SAB. 14	9:00 P.M.
DOM. 15	5:00 P.M. y
	8:00 P.M.

CASA BEETHOVEN
MAGATZEM DE MUSICA
PARTITURES NACIONALS I ESTRANGERES
RAMBLES.97 (LA VIRREINA) · TEL.301 48 26
BARCELONA. 2

La música suave calma el apetito

WEATHER AND SEASONS
El tiempo y las estaciones

¿Qué tiempo hace?   How's the weather?

Hace buen tiempo.   Más o menos.   Hace mal tiempo.

Hace sol.	It's sunny.	Hace fresco.	It's cool.	Hace frío.	It's cold.
Hace calor.	It's warm.	Hace viento.	It's windy.	Relampaguea.	There's lightning.
		Está húmedo.	It's humid.	Nieva.	It's snowing.
		Está nublado.	It's cloudy.	Truena.	It's thundering.
				Llueve.	It's raining.

¿En qué estación estamos?   What's the season?
Estamos en...   It's ....

Las cuatro estaciones

la primavera

el otoño

el invierno

el verano

When "en" is used before a season, omit "el" or "la."

 A mal tiempo, buena cara.

A smile brightens a cloudy day.

Exercises

A ¿Qué frase corresponde a cada dibujo?

1. _____   a. Hace sol.

2. _____   b. Relampaguea.

3. _____   c. Llueve.

4. _____   d. Hace viento.

5. _____   e. Hace frío.

B ¿Qué tiempo hace? Contesta la pregunta en español.

1. _____

2. _____

3. _____

4. _____

5. _____

C ¿Qué estación corresponde a cada dibujo?

1. _____   a. verano

2. _____   b. inviernc

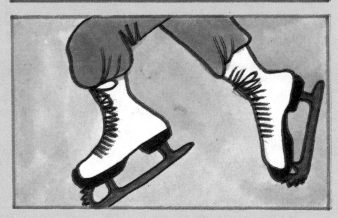

3. _____   c. primavera

4. _____   d. otoño

D In **column 1**, write the English meaning of each Spanish word. When you have finished the entire column, cover the column of words at the left, and in **column 2**, change the English words into Spanish.

<table>
<tr><td></td><td>**column 1**
(English)</td><td>**column 2**
(Spanish)</td></tr>
<tr><td>1. sol</td><td></td><td></td></tr>
<tr><td>2. relámpago</td><td></td><td></td></tr>
<tr><td>3. primavera</td><td></td><td></td></tr>
<tr><td>4. verano</td><td></td><td></td></tr>
<tr><td>5. tiempo</td><td></td><td></td></tr>
<tr><td>6. otoño</td><td></td><td></td></tr>
<tr><td>7. estación</td><td></td><td></td></tr>
<tr><td>8. fresco</td><td></td><td></td></tr>
<tr><td>9. calor</td><td></td><td></td></tr>
<tr><td>10. Llueve.</td><td></td><td></td></tr>
<tr><td>11. invierno</td><td></td><td></td></tr>
<tr><td>12. mal</td><td></td><td></td></tr>
<tr><td>13. trueno</td><td></td><td></td></tr>
<tr><td>14. frío</td><td></td><td></td></tr>
</table>

E Asocia la columna **A** con la columna **B**.

A	B
1. lluvia _____	a. hacer sol
2. nieve _____	b. tronar
3. trueno _____	c. relampaguear
4. relámpago _____	d. nevar
5. sol _____	e. llover

F ¿Qué tiempo hace? *Using the cue at the left, write a statement about the weather.* (En español, por favor.)

1. (mittens and parka) _____.

2. (umbrella) _____.

3. (sunglasses) _____.

4. (snowflakes) _____.

5. (lightning bolts) _____.

6. (air conditioner) _____.

7. (cardigan sweater) _____.

8. (sailboat) _____.

9. (outdoor tennis court) _____.

10. (rain, wind, and hail) _____.

G Lee el párrafo. Escoge las respuestas correctas.

Las cuatro estaciones

En primavera hace fresco y llueve mucho. Todo está verde. En verano hace mucho calor. Hace sol casi todos los días. En otoño hace fresco y hace mucho viento. En invierno hace frío y nieva mucho. Las cuatro estaciones son interesantes.

> **todo** = everything

1. El invierno es...
    a. caluroso.   b. verde.
    c. frío.   d. rojo.

2. En primavera todo está...
    a. verde.   b. caluroso.
    c. interesante.   d. frío.

3. Hace fresco en...
    a. verano.   b. invierno.
    c. primavera y otoño.   d. Madrid.

4. Hay...estaciones.
    a. seis   b. tres
    c. cuatro   d. catorce

Crucigrama

H

Vertical

1. cooler than cool
2. "...buen tiempo."
3. light and heat source
4. what skiers like to say
7. when the storm speaks
8. season of roses
9. Summer is a "..." of the year.
11. when it's cold and snowy
12. "Hace mal...."

Horizontal

1. slightly "frío"
4. "Está...."
5. harvest season (*temperate zone*)
6. when showers fall
10. when the sky sparkles and blazes
13. "A mal tiempo, buena...."
14. "En marzo hace...."
15. nature's rebirth
16. damp and clammy
17. opposite of "frío"

CONDICIONES GENERALES

El ambiente se manifiesta fresco en horas de la noche; cálido y húmedo en horas del día y que trae como consecuencia la formación de áreas de tormentas eléctricas con lluvia.

MANIFIESTESE CON LAS ESTACIONES.

TEMPERATURA | **CLIMA**

CENTIGRADOS

38°

El tiempo en el mundo

CIUDAD	MAX	MIN	COND.
Amsterdam	18	13	Nuboso
Bruselas	19	15	Nuboso
Ginebra	22	18	Nuboso
Londres	20	14	Nuboso
Moscú	23	15	Nuboso
Nueva York	26	20	Nuboso
París	19	9	Despejado
Río de Janeiro	22	16	Nuboso
Roma	29	17	Despejado
Tokio	26	22	Nuboso
Varsovia	20	16	Nuboso
Viena	28	16	Nuboso
Washington	31	25	Nuboso

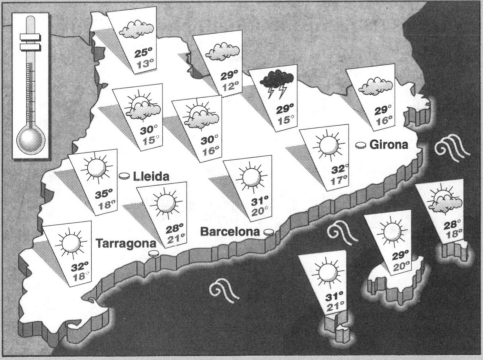

SOLEADO   NUBLADO

NUBOSO   CUBIERTO

LLUVIA   TORMENTA

NIEVE   NIEBLA

BRUMAS   M. RIZADA

MAREJADILLA   MAREJADA

15°
-6°
Temperaturas
Máxima y mínima
previstas para hoy

¿Qué día es hoy?
Hoy es...

What day is today?
Today is. . . .

Monday lunes	martes	miércoles	jueves	viernes	sábado	domingo
	1	2	3	4	5	6
7	8	9	10	11	12	13
14	15	16	17	18	19	20
21	22	23	24	25	26	27
28	29	30	31			

¿Cuál es la fecha de hoy?
  Es el primero de mayo.
  el dos de julio.
  el doce de octubre.
  17- 3 - 95.

What is the date today?
  It's May first.
  July second.
  October 12.
  3 -17- 95.

Hoy por ti,
mañana por mí.

Every dog has his day.

Cuaderno de Nilda
Estudia para el examen de inglés:

1. tomorrow   (mi cumpleaños)
2. the day after tomorrow
3. yesterday
4. the day before yesterday
5. the day
6. the holiday (¡Bravo!)
7. the school day
8. the birthday (mañana)
9. the week
10. the weekend (¡mi vida!)
11. the month

Nilda's Notebook
study for English test:

1. mañana
2. pasado mañana
3. ayer
4. anteayer
5. el día
6. la fiesta
7. el día escolar
8. el cumpleaños
9. la semana
10. el fin de semana
11. el mes

Weekdays and Mythology

Derivations and Comparisons

Spanish Day	Roman Mythology
lunes	day honoring the moon god "luna" = moon
martes	day honoring the god of war, Mars
miércoles	day honoring Mercury, messenger of the gods
jueves	day honoring Jupiter or Jove, father and king of the gods
viernes	day honoring Venus, goddess of love
sábado	day honoring Saturn, god of the harvest and agriculture
domingo	day honoring "the Lord" "dominus" = the Lord Christian conversion of "solis dies" "solis dies" = day of the sun

Exercises

A Write in numerical form the dates your teacher reads.

1. _____

2. _____

3. _____

4. _____

5. _____

REMINDER: Where did you put the number for the day? _____

B Label the current month. Include the names of the days and all the numbers.

MES _____

DÍA	DÍA	DÍA	DÍA	DÍA	DÍA	DÍA

C Escribe las fechas.

1. Tuesday, April 1st _____

2. Wednesday, May 2nd _____

3. Thursday, September 16th _____

4. Friday, July 26th _____

5. Sunday, March 17th _____

D Asocia el inglés con el español.

1. hoy _____   a. yesterday

2. anteayer _____   b. the day after tomorrow

3. pasado mañana _____   c. today

4. ayer _____   d. tomorrow

5. mañana _____   e. the day before yesterday

E Escribe en español.

1. the first month of the year _____

2. the day that usually begins the school week _____

3. a windy month *en primavera* _____

4. the day on which Thanksgiving is celebrated _____

5. the month in which school ends _____

6. the last day of the week _____

7. the month of U.S. independence _____

8. the month in which Columbus Day is celebrated _____

9. the month in which *otōno* ends _____

10. the month in which Valentine's Day is celebrated _____

F Escribe el día en español, según el dibujo.

1. _____

2. _____

3. _____

4. _____

5. _____

6. _____

7. _____

G Lee el párrafo. Escoge las respuestas correctas.

La corrida de toros es un famoso espectáculo español. Hay una corrida cada domingo. Hoy es domingo y es también el cumpleaños de Pepe. El asiste con su familia a la corrida en Málaga. Es su regalo de cumpleaños. El matador entra con su cuadrilla y marcha alrededor de la plaza de toros. La música comienza y todo el mundo grita, "¡Olé!" Con su traje de luces y sombrero de tres picos, el matador es una figura muy impresionante. Entra el toro y la corrida comienza. ¡Qué día más divertido!

> **la corrida de toros** = the bullfight
> **la plaza de toros** = the bullfighting stadium
> **cada** = each
> **el regalo** = the present
> **matador** = the bullfighter
> **la cuadrilla** = team of assistants
> **el pico** = the peak
> **divertido** = enjoyable
> **alrededor de** = around

1. Una diversión popular de España es . . . .
    a. la plaza de toros   b. el béisbol
    c. la corrida de toros   d. Pepe
2. Un grito típico de la corrida es . . .
    a. ¡No más!   b. ¡Qué le vaya bien!
    c. ¡Mátelo!   d. ¡Olé!
3. El matador lleva . . . .
    a. un abrigo   b. un traje de luces
    c. una sonrisa   d. un sombrero de jipijapa
4. Es el . . . de Pepe.
    a. feria   b. toro
    c. cumpleaños   d. padre
5. La corrida de toros es . . . .
    a. en Málaga   b. en México
    c. en Madrid   d. en La Habana

Crucigrama

Vertical

1. first full month of spring
2. month noted for its wind
3. harvest month
4. month named for Julius Caesar
6. month that begins the year
7. autumn month of thirty days
9. day before "domingo"
10. last month of the year
13. last day of the school week
15. Seven of these make a week.

Horizontal

2. month that "brings flowers"
4. Jove's day
5. last full month of winter
8. month that follows "mayo"
11. yesterday's tomorrow
12. month in which classes resume
14. precedes "martes"
16. "día. . .(of school)"
17. "enero," "mayo," "junio," etc.

Five Great Authors

Miguel de Cervantes, the author of Spain's most beloved novel, *Don Quijote de la Mancha*, was born in Alcalá de Henares in 1547. He lived a life almost as unbelievable as that of his famous character. Cervantes was a wanderer, a soldier, a prisoner of pirates, a disgraced public official, a mediocre poet and dramatist, and finally, Spain's most famous novelist. Fighting against the Turks, he lost the use of his left hand at the battle of Lepanto. While returning to Spain from this battle, he was captured by pirates who made him a prisoner and sent him to the galleys. Five years later Cervantes escaped from his captors and returned home. Upon arriving, he was appointed mayor of his town. Later, when money was found missing from the town's account, he spent time in jail. He left in disgrace after his release. Cervantes tried writing both poems and plays with little success. He also wrote novels. In 1615 he published *Don Quijote de la Mancha*, which was an immediate success and led to great honor. His *Novelas ejemplares*, twelve short novels, are still considered masterpieces of Spanish prose. Cervantes died in 1616.

Don Quijote de la Mancha is a satirical novel about a nobleman, don Quijote. The hero is driven mad by his excessive reading of novels of chivalry. Full of noble ideals, don Quijote sets out in quest of good deeds to perform, fair maidens to rescue, and vicious dragons to slay. Accompanied by his squire, Sancho Panza, he has many misadventures that are quite humorous to the reader and quite unpleasant for the hero. Don Quijote is finally sobered by the results of his misadventures and vows never to read such stories again. The modern musical, *Man of la Mancha*, is based on this famous work.

Gustavo Adolfo Bécquer (1836–70) was one of Spain's great romantic poets. He was born in Seville but moved to Madrid at the age of eighteen. It was there, in the capital, that this young poet hoped to achieve literary fame. However, both he and his brother Valeriano, an artist, earned only a meager living writing verse and selling paintings. It was said that both brothers existed more on ideals than on nourishment. They died in poverty in 1870.

Quien bien anda, bien acaba.   All's well that ends well.

Bécquer's most famous poems are found in the collection *Rimas*, published in 1871. These poems are considered models of romantic verse. Bécquer's poetry is personal, sentimental, free, rebellious, and wild. Its themes are escape, piracy, love, and idealism. His verse is very musical and creates feelings of happiness and sympathy. Students of Spanish literature study this poetry seriously.

Rubén Darío was the pen name of Félix Rubén García Saramiento, one of Latin America's greatest lyric poets. Born in Melapa, Nicaragua, Darío displayed a talent for writing and pursued a career in journalism. He obtained a job as a reporter for *La Nación*, Argentina's most respected newspaper. As its foreign bureau chief, Darío traveled to Chile, France, Spain, and Italy. He quickly mastered French and Italian and made friends with the poets of these lands. Darío was greatly influenced by the French poets. In 1904 he was appointed diplomatic minister to Brazil. He held a similar post in Spain from 1908 to 1911. Darío was recognized for his poetic talent and lectured on poetry and the arts in Europe, South America, and the United States. He was greatly concerned with the freedom of his tiny republic and quite upset with the role of the United States in the internal affairs of Nicaragua. He voiced his concerns in a poem entitled *Oda a Roosevelt*. Many of Darío's poems have patriotic themes. He died of pneumonia in 1916.

Darío's poetry was "New World" in style. He employed in a modern manner all he had learned from the classical writers and the modern poets of Europe. His poems greatly influenced future writers of Spanish poetry. He published his first book of poems, *Azul*, in 1888, and the critics praised it highly. *Cantos de vida y esperanza* and *Prosas profanas* were published next. This outstanding poet blended ideas with color and electrifying sound. To honor his artistic achievement, his country has renamed Melapa. It is now Ciudad Darío.

Emilia Bazán (1852-1921) is known as one of Spain's outstanding novelists. Bazán was a countess, the only daughter of Count Pardo Bazán. She was a child prodigy and could read and write well by age four. Historical practices and traditions had made it difficult for most women to be well educated, but changes in the late nineteenth and early twentieth centuries provided increased opportunities for women authors. Bazán took advantage of the opportunities. By age fourteen she was writing scholarly commentaries on the *Bible*, the *Iliad*, the *Divine Comedy*, and other great works.

Bazán introduced "naturalism" into her novels. Naturalism views human beings as part of nature. Each person is, therefore, subject to nature's two great forces, heredity and environment. The people in Bazán's novels struggle with these forces.

Bazán loved her native province of Galicia and spent her summer there every year. Her novels use Galicia for their setting and are models of fine description, skillful plots, and understanding of people. *Los pazos de Ulloa* and *La madre naturaleza* are her two finest novels. The author was prominent in the cause of women's rights and chaired the Department for Literature at the University of Madrid.

Carmen Laforet (1921-) was born in Barcelona. Her father was an outgoing athlete and sportsman who excelled in cycling and shooting. He was also a successful architect. Her mother was religious, caring, and gentle. Laforet seemed to inherit all of her parents' good qualities. She was only thirteen when her mother died, which grieved her greatly. The coldness of her stepmother did little to lighten her sorrow.

After high school Laforet studied first the liberal arts and then law at the university. She abandoned her studies, however, and turned to writing. She was immediately successful. In 1944, at 23, she published her novel, *Nada*. It won Spain's highest honor for the novel, the *Premio Eugenio Nadal*. *La isla y los demonios*, published in 1952, confirmed her outstanding literary skill. Her novel *La mujer nueva* won the *Premio Menorca* in 1955 and the *Premio Miguel de Cervantes* in 1956.

The author introduced "spiritualism" into the novel. Spiritualism is a theory that sees people as more than material beings. According to this theory, a human being must respect nature but look for total happiness beyond material things. In the novel *Nada*, Andrea, the main character, is deeply moved by the meaningless lives of those about her. She comes away from her experiences more understanding, more serious, and ready to look beyond the material for solutions to life's problems.

Exercises

A Guess who...

1. was a galley slave. _____

2. wrote about pirates. _____

3. was a child prodigy. _____

4. was a reporter. _____

5. was born in Nicaragua. _____

6. was injured in the battle of Lepanto. _____

7. studied the arts and law. _____

B Asocia el inglés con el español.

A	**B**
1. Sancho Panza _____	a. Latin American poet
2. Bécquer _____	b. Spain's greatest author
3. Rubén Darío _____	c. poems by Bécquer
4. Cervantes _____	d. a poet who died young
5. *Rimas* _____	e. a character created by Cervantes

C Write the full name of the author of each work listed below.

1. *Nada* _____

2. *Azul* _____

3. *Rimas* _____

4. *Don Quijote de la Mancha* _____

5. *Prosas profanas* _____

6. *Novelas ejemplares* _____

7. *La madre naturaleza* _____

D Complete the analogies.

1. _____ : novel = Bécquer: poem

2. Cervantes: chivalry = _____ : piracy

3. Darío: _____ = Bécquer: Spain

4. Rubén: Darío = Miguel : _____

5. satire: _____ = patriotism: Darío

6. naturalism: Bazán = spiritualism: _____

¿Qué nombre corresponde a cada dibujo?

Cervantes

Darío

Bécquer

F Which writer would most likely...

1. be an expert on art? _____

2. guide friends through Galicia? _____

3. prefer to travel only on land? _____

4. discuss poetry at a French café? _____

5. appreciate fine architecture? _____

6. laugh at himself? _____

7. object strenuously if a foreign country were to take advantage of his people?

   _____

G Label each plot described below as classical, modern, or romantic.

1. Paco Ramírez decides to avenge himself against an unjust government that stole his farm. He enlists a band of rebels and flees to the mountains to plan a revolution.

   _____

2. Doña Elvira decides to abandon her plans to marry don Franco whom she greatly loves. Her decision springs from her sense of familial duty, which requires her to remain at home to care for her aged parents.

   _____

3. In the lyric "The Orange-Smelling Field," the one-eyed leaf spies on the purple odor who lives in the grove of white water vapors. All is reported to Doctor Colorsmell.

   _____

H Completa las frases.

1. _____ was a poet who lived in dire poverty.

2. _____'s birthplace was renamed for him.

3. _____ and _____were two great poets.

4. _____ was a great novelist.

5. _____, _____,
   _____ and _____ were all from Spain.

6. _____ was from Latin America.

7. _____ had a brother who was an artist.

8. _____ served as mayor of his town.

9. _____ represented his nation in Europe.

10. _____ was a wounded war hero.

18

LEISURE AND RECREATION
El tiempo libre y las diversiones

¿Adónde vas tú?
Where are you going?

Voy al partido.
I'm going to the game.

Voy al museo.
I'm going to the museum.

Voy a la fiesta.
I'm going to the party.

Voy a la playa.
I'm going to the beach.

Marcos:	¿Adónde vas tú esta noche?	Where are you going tonight?
Tomás:	Voy al partido.	I'm going to the game.
Marcos:	¡Yo también!	Me, too!

✻✻✻✻✻✻

Andrés:	¿Adónde vas tú hoy?	Where are you going today?
Patricia:	Voy al museo...al Museo del Prado.*	I'm going to the museum...to the Prado Museum.
Andrés:	¿Por qué?	Why?
Patricia:	Para ver la exhibición de Goya.	To see the Goya exhibit.

The Prado, Spain's most prominent art museum, is located in Madrid.

En la variedad está el gusto.   Variety is the spice of life.

Juego al volibol.
I play volleyball.

Juego al fútbol.
I play soccer.

¿ Qué deportes haces tú ?
What sports do you play?

Juego al tenis.
I play tennis.

Juego al básquetbol.
I play basketball.

Juego al béisbol.
I play baseball.

¿Qué te gusta hacer?
What do you like to do?

Me gusta esquiar.
I like skiing.

Me gusta leer.
I like reading.

Me gusta bailar.
I like dancing.

Me gusta montar a caballo.
I like horseback riding.

Me gusta nadar.
I like swimming.

Me gusta montar en bicicleta.
I like biking.

Susana:	Mañana hay un picnic.	There's a picnic tomorrow.
Juanita:	¿Dónde?	Where?
Susana:	En la playa. ¿Quieres ir conmigo?	At the beach. Do you want to go with me?
Juanita:	Sí. Me encanta nadar.	Yes. I love swimming.

❀❀❀❀❀

Lucía:	¿Vas a la fiesta esta noche?	Are you going to the party tonight?
Daniel:	Claro. Va a haber música, ¿verdad?	Of course. There'll be music, won't there?
Lucía:	Sí. Me encanta bailar.	Yes. I love dancing.

Exercises

A ¿Adónde vas tú? Completa cada frase en español.

1. Voy al _____ . (*game*)

2. Voy a un _____ . (*picnic*)

3. Voy a la _____ . (*party*)

4. Voy al _____ . (*museum*)

5. Voy a la _____ . (*beach*)

B Select the correct answers based on the previous dialogues.

1. ¿Cuándo es el partido?
   a. mañana   b. viernes
   c. esta noche   d. a las ocho

2. ¿Qué es el Prado?
   a. un caballo   b. un partido
   c. una exhibición de Goya   d. un museo

3. ¿Quién es Goya?
   a. un profesor   b. un pintor
   c. un museo   d. un actor

4. ¿Cuándo es el picnic?
   a. mañana   b. hoy
   c. en la playa   d. yo también

5. ¿Dónde es el picnic?
   a. a la fiesta   b. al Prado
   c. al béisbol   d. en la playa

C ¿Qué deportes haces tú? Completa cada frase en español.

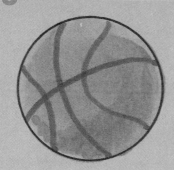

1. Juego al _____ .

2. Juego al _____ .

3. Juego al _____ .

4. Juego al _____ .

5. Juego al _____ .

Unit 18 *Leisure and Recreation*   127

D Descifra las palabras.

1. TARDIOP _____

2. CPIINC _____

3. YPLAA _____

4. SAIFET _____

5. USOME _____

E ¿Qué te gusta hacer? Completa cada frase en español.

1. Me gusta _____ .

2. Me gusta _____ .

3. Me gusta _____ .

4. Me gusta _____ .

5. Me gusta _____ .

6. Me gusta _____ .

F   Completa el diálogo en español.

Mónica: ¿Adónde _____ tú hoy?

Patricia: Voy _____ la playa. ¿Quieres _____ conmigo?

Mónica: _____ . Me encanta el océano.

Patricia: ¿Qué _____ haces tú en la playa?

Mónica: Me gusta _____ en el océano y

_____ al volibol.

G   Lee el párrafo. Escoge las respuestas correctas.

Dolores organiza una fiesta pequeña en la playa. Ella invita a sus amigos Yolanda, Felipe, Juan Carlos, Rosario y Guillermo a la fiesta. La fiesta comienza a las tres. Hace buen tiempo hoy porque hace calor y no está nublado. A los amigos les gusta nadar en el océano y jugar al volibol. Después de las actividades, va a haber un picnic con sandwiches de jamón y de pollo, salchichas, bebidas y helados. ¡La fiesta en la playa va a ser magnífica!

> **les gusta** = (they) like
> **después de** = after
> **va a ser** = is going to be

1. ¿Quién va a la fiesta de Dolores?
   a. sus padres
   c. sus hermanas
   b. sus amigos
   d. sus tíos

2. ¿A qué hora comienza la fiesta?
   a. a la playa
   c. a las tres
   b. a medianoche
   d. a las doce menos diez

3. ¿Qué tiempo hace?
   a. Hace buen tiempo.
   c. Nieva.
   b. Llueve.
   d. Hace frío.

4. ¿Qué les gusta a los amigos?
   a. Les gusta bailar.
   c. Les gusta nadar y jugar al volibol.
   b. Les gusta jugar al fútbol.
   d. Les gusta montar a caballo.

5. ¿Qué comida va a haber en el picnic?
   a. una playa
   c. unos sandwiches
   b. un restaurante
   d. un vaso

SHOPPING
Las compras

Ana:	¿Adónde vas tú?	Where are you going?
Federico:	Al centro comercial.	To the shopping center.
Ana:	¿Qué vas a comprar?	What are you going to buy?
Federico:	Unos tenis.	Some athletic shoes.

❀❀❀❀❀

Vendedor:	Buenos días, señora. ¿En qué puedo servirle?	Hello, Ma'am. May I help you?
Clienta:	Estoy mirando, nada más. Gracias.	I'm just looking. Thanks.

 Al que llegue primero, se le sirve primero. First come, first served.

Cliente:	¿Cuánto cuesta este CD?	How much is this CD?
Cajera:	Cuesta 28,00 pesos.	It costs 28 pesos.
Cliente:	¡Es un poco caro!	That's a little expensive!
Cajera:	No, es barato.	No, it's cheap.
Cliente:	Está bien. Lo compro. Aquí está el dinero, señorita.	OK. I'll buy it. Here's the money, Miss.
Cajera:	Muchas gracias. Aquí está el cambio.	Thank you very much. Here's your change.

| Vendedora: | ¿Algo más? | Anything else? |
| Cliente: | Pues, tres tomates, cinco duraznos y unas habichuelas. Sí, eso es todo. | Uhm...three tomatoes, five peaches and some green beans. Yes, that's all. |

Exercises

A Asocia la columna **A** con la columna **B**.

<table>
<tr><td align="center">A</td><td></td><td align="center">B</td></tr>
<tr><td>1. tenis</td><td>_____</td><td>a. market</td></tr>
<tr><td>2. habichuelas</td><td>_____</td><td>b. shoe store</td></tr>
<tr><td>3. CD</td><td>_____</td><td>c. furniture store</td></tr>
<tr><td>4. silla</td><td>_____</td><td>d. stationery store</td></tr>
<tr><td>5. bolígrafos y cuadernos</td><td>_____</td><td>e. music store</td></tr>
</table>

B Completa cada frase en español, según la ilustración.

1. Me encantan los _____.

2. La señora Blanca escoje unas frutas buenas en

   el _____ .

3. Hago mis compras en el

   _____ .

4. Aquí está el _____ ,
   señor.

5. El CD es barato. _____
   19,00 pesos.

C Choose the expression from the following list that completes each sentence correctly.

barato   pesos   comprar

caja   compras

Alicia hace sus _____ en la tienda. Ella va a

_____ un CD de música clásica. Este CD cuesta

21,00 _____ . No es caro. Es

_____ . Ella va a la

_____ con su CD.

D Contesta las preguntas en español.

1. If you see the sign "Ofertas," how would you expect the price of the object to be?
   a. barato
   b. el dinero
   c. caro
   d. la moneda

2. What do you reply if the cashier says "Cuesta 40,00 pesos"?
   a. Aquí está el dinero.
   b. ¿Dónde está la tienda?
   c. ¿Cuánto cuesta?
   d. Gracias, eso es todo.

3. What do you get back if you give the cashier too much money?
   a. la caja
   b. el cambio
   c. barato
   d. unas habichuelas

4. Who helps you find what you need?
   a. el dinero
   b. el vendedor
   c. la cajera
   d. la clienta

5. What do you say if you don't need the salesclerk's help right now?
   a. ¿En qué puedo servirle?
   b. ¡Es un poco caro!
   c. Estoy mirando, nada más.
   d. ¿Algo más?

E   Escoje la respuesta correcta.

1. ¿Eso es todo?
   a. No, es caro.
   c. No, es barato.
   b. No, pues, unos duraznos, por favor.
   d. No, estoy mirando, nada más.

2. ¿Por qué vas tú a la tienda?
   a. No tengo sed.
   c. Hay un picnic.
   b. Llevo una bata.
   d. Yo hago mis compras.

3. ¿Son baratos los tenis?
   a. Sí, aquí está el cambio.
   c. No, son caros.
   b. No, es el vendedor.
   d. Sí, eso es todo.

4. ¿Cuánto cuesta el CD?
   a. Cuesta 24,00 pesos.
   c. Eso es todo.
   b. Pues, estoy mirando, nada más.
   d. En el centro comercial.

5. ¿Qué vas a comprar?
   a. ofertas
   c. unos tomates y unas habichuelas
   b. un vendedor
   d. el cambio

F   Tomás is shopping in a clothing store. Complete his conversation with the salesclerk.

Vendedor: Buenos días, señor. ¿En qué puedo

_____ ?

Tomás: Estoy _____ , nada más. Gracias.

Vendedor: Hay muchas ofertas. Todo está _____ :

las camisas, los pantalones, los abrigos y los zapatos.

Tomás: Gracias, señor. Pues, ¿ _____ cuesta este

pantalón negro?

Vendedor: _____ 70,00 pesos. Es barato, ¿verdad?

Tomás: No, es un poco _____ . No puedo

_____ el pantalón. Tengo 35,00 pesos,

_____ más.

Crucigrama

G

Vertical

1. a female customer
2. the opposite of "barato"
3. "¿Algo...?"
5. compact disc
7. "¿En qué puedo...?"
9. where you buy fresh vegetables
10. "¿...vas tú?"
11. "Eso es...." (all)

Horizontal

1. a cash register
4. a long, thin, green vegetable
6. a female salesclerk
8. a shopping center
12. "Al que llegue..., se le sirve primero."
13. what you pay your bill with
14. "Estoy mirando,...más."
15. fruit that has a fuzzy exterior
16. sporty "zapatos"

Los viajes y los medios de transporte

¿Cómo viajas tú?

How do you travel?

Yo viajo en avión.
I travel by plane.

Yo viajo en autobús.
I travel by bus.

Yo viajo en carro.
I travel by car.

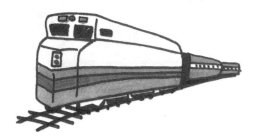

Yo viajo en tren.
I travel by train.

Yo viajo en barco.
I travel by ship.

 Viajando se instruye la gente. Whoever travels far knows much.

Empleada:	¿Su pasaporte, señor?	Your passport, Sir?
Viajero:	Está en mi maleta, señorita.	It's in my suitcase, Miss.
Empleada:	Pero Ud. debe tenerlo consigo...y especialmente en el control de pasaportes, al llegar.	But you must have it on you...and especially at passport control upon arrival.
Viajero:	De acuerdo. Espere Ud..... ¿Y dónde abordamos nosotros?	OK. Wait.... And where do we board?
Empleada:	En la puerta 20, a la derecha.	At gate 20, on your right.

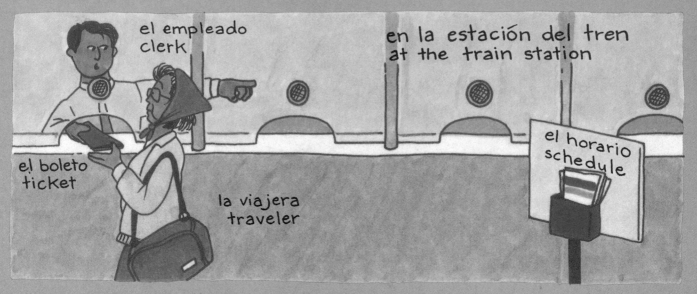

Viajera:	Señor, ¿a qué hora sale el siguiente tren para Madrid?	What time does the next train for Madrid leave, Sir?
Empleado:	Al mediodía, señora. Aquí está el horario.	At noon, Ma'am. Here's the schedule.
Viajera:	Bueno, pues, me gustaría comprar un boleto de ida y vuelta de segunda clase.	Good, then I'd like a round-trip ticket in second class.
Empleado:	Aquí está el boleto. Son 3.000,00 pesetas.	Here's the ticket. It's 3,000 pesetas.

| Sr. León: | Señora...¿cómo puedo llegar al hotel Ritz? | Ma'am...how do I get to the Ritz Hotel? |
| Sra. Jurado: | Tome Ud. el autobús número 2 y bájese Ud. en la oficina de correos. El hotel está a la izquierda. | Take bus number 2 and get off at the post office. The hotel is on the left. |

Ejercicios

A Match the English with the Spanish.

1. Espere Ud. _____
2. me gustaría _____
3. a la izquierda _____
4. Bájese en la oficina _____
   de correos.
5. ¿Dónde abordamos? _____
6. Tome Ud. el autobús. _____
7. un boleto de ida y vuelta _____
8. Ud. debe tenerlo consigo. _____
9. Aquí está el horario. _____
10. a la derecha _____

a. a round-trip ticket

b. on the right

c. Where do we board?

d. Here's the schedule.

e. Get off at the post office.

f. You must have it on you.

g. Wait.

h. I would like

i. Take the bus.

j. on the left

B ¿Cómo viajas tú? Completa cada frase en español.

1. Yo viajo _____ .

2. Yo viajo _____ .

3. Yo viajo _____ .

4. Yo viajo _____ .

5. Yo viajo _____ .

C Contesta las preguntas en español.

1. Where do you go to take a train?
   a. al aeropuerto
   b. en el control de pasaportes
   c. a la estación del tren
   d. en la calle

2. What do you ask if you want directions to the train station?
   a. ¿Y dónde abordamos?
   b. ¿Cómo puedo llegar a la estación del tren?
   c. ¿A qué hora sale el tren?
   d. ¿En qué puedo servirle?

3. What would you look at to find the times when trains, buses, planes, etc. arrive and leave?
   a. el horario
   b. el mostrador
   c. el pasaporte
   d. la maleta

4. What would you say if you wanted to buy a ticket?
   a. Aquí está mi pasaporte.
   b. Me gustaría comprar un boleto.
   c. ¿Adónde vas tú?
   d. ¿Cómo puedo llegar a la oficina de correos?

5. If you don't want a first-class ticket, what do you say?
   a. un boleto de ida y vuelta
   b. un boleto
   c. el autobús número 2
   d. de segunda

D Decifra las palabras.

1. ATSRROMDO _____

2. ROHIRAO _____

3. ORNCOLT ED STEPRAASOP

   _____

4. JOVERIA _____

5. PRATOSPAE _____

E   Lee el párrafo. Escoje las respuestas correctas.

Hace buen tiempo hoy. Adán y Patricio están en la estación del tren. Van a viajar
en tren. Adán va a comprar dos boletos para ir a Barcelona. Los abuelos de Adán
viven cerca de Barcelona. Los dos amigos esperan el tren en el andén número 4. El
tren llega a la estación a las catorce horas. Cuando llega, ellos abordan el tren. Adán
escoge un asiento cerca de la ventana. Los amigos hablan de su visita a Barcelona
donde hay mucho que hacer. Están felices. Al llegar, toman el autobús para ir a la
casa de los abuelos de Adán.

> **cerca de** = near
> **esperan** = they wait for
> **andén** = platform
> **llega** = arrives
> **asiento** = seat

1. ¿Dónde están Adán y Patricio?
   a. en el aeropuerto   b. en el autobús
   c. en el taxi   d. en la estación del tren

2. ¿Adónde viajan Adán y Patricio hoy?
   a. a Sevilla   b. a Barcelona
   c. a Córdoba   d. a Santiago

3. ¿Cuántos boletos compra Adán?
   a. dos   b. uno
   c. catorce   d. cuatro

4. ¿Dónde esperan el tren?
   a. cerca de la ventana   b. en el mostrador
   c. en el andén número 4   d. en las maletas

5. ¿Cómo van ellos a la casa de los abuelos de Adán?
   a. en avión   b. en autobús
   c. en carro   d. en barco

F   Complete the analogies.

1. empleado: _____ = viajero: viajera

2. avión: aeropuerto = tren: _____

3. barco: océano = autobús: _____

4. empleado: _____ = profesor: escritorio

5. uno: dos = primero: _____

Crucigrama

Vertical

1. wait
3. where
4. good
6. what you show at passport control
9. "El siguiente tren...Barcelona sale al mediodía."
12. "...Ud. en la oficina de correos."
13. a plane
15. "El tren...al mediodía."

Horizontal

2. "Un boleto de...y vuelta."
5. "Mi pasaporte...en mi maleta."
7. a street
8. a female clerk
10. means of traveling on water
11. "¿Y dónde...?"
14. a female traveler
16. "¿Cómo puedo...al hotel Ritz?"
17. "...3.000,00 pesetas."
18. opposite of "izquierda"
19. "Yo viajo...tren."

G

1 VIAJE
SISTEMA DE TRANSPORTE COLECTIVO
METRO
CIUDAD DE MEXICO
PB·VI

Frecuenta

NOMBRE
DIRECCION
TELEFONO
No. de Socio Frecuenta

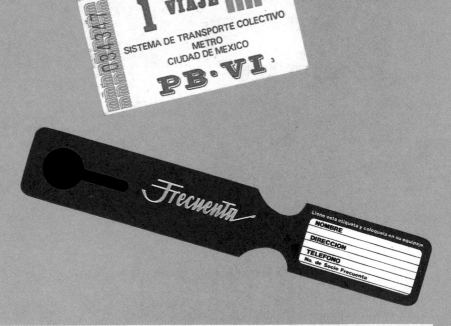

HORARIOS

TREN PUNTA

TREN LLANO

TREN VALLE

	P	V	LL	P	LL
	○	○	○	○	○
MADRID - CHAMARTIN	11,00	12,00	14,00	16,00	22,05
GUADALAJARA	11,31	12,31	—	—	22,50
ZARAGOZA	14,13	15,32	16,59	18,59	2,00
LLEIDA	15,58	—	18,38	20,35	—
TARRAGONA	17,15	18,43	—	—	5,32
BARCELONA SANTS	18,30	20,00	20,35	22,35	7,00
BARCELONA FRANÇA	—	20,20	20,55	22,55	—

	LL	V	P	P	LL
	○	○	○	○	○
BARCELONA FRANÇA	8,05	9,35	—	15,05	—
BARCELONA SANTS	8,30	10,00	12,00	15,30	22,00
TARRAGONA	—	11,02	13,02	—	23,18
LLEIDA	10,17	—	14,11	17,15	—
ZARAGOZA	12,00	14,00	16,00	19,00	2,47
GUADALAJARA	—	17,00	18,47	—	6,40
MADRID-CHAMARTIN	15,05	17,45	19,30	22,10	7,45

○ DIARIO.
NOTA: ADEMAS DE ESTOS SERVICIOS, DISPONEN DEL TRENHOTEL «ANTONO GAUDI» CON SALIDA DE { MADRID-CHAMARTIN / BARCELONA } A LAS 23,10 Y LLEGADA A { BARCELONA / MADRID-CHAMARTIN } A LAS 8,00 HORAS.